HISTORY, CULTURE, AND REGION IN SOUTHEAST ASIAN PERSPECTIVES

HISTORY, CULTURE, AND REGION IN SOUTHEAST ASIAN PERSPECTIVES

O.W. WOLTERS

INSTITUTE OF SOUTHEAST ASIAN STUDIES

The **Institute of Southeast Asian Studies** was established as an autonomous organization in May 1968. It is a regional research centre for scholars and other specialists concerned with modern Southeast Asia. The Institute's research interest is focused on the many-faceted problems of development and modernization, and political and social change in Southeast Asia.

The Institute is governed by a twenty-two-member Board of Trustees on which are represented the National University of Singapore, appointees from the government, as well as representatives from a broad range of professional and civic organizations and groups. A ten-man Executive Committee oversees day-to-day operations; it is chaired by the Director, the Institute's chief academic and administrative officer.

The responsibility for facts and opinions expressed in this publication rests exclusively with the author and his interpretations do not necessarily reflect the views or the policy of the Institute or its supporters.

Published in 1982 by the
Institute of Southeast Asian Studies
Heng Mui Keng Terrace, Pasir Panjang
Singapore 0511

ISBN 9971-902-42-7
Printed by LOLITHO PTE LTD

In Memoriam
John M. Echols
1913 – 1982

Contents

Introduction

A shorter and somewhat different version of this paper was presented at a seminar held in Manila in June 1980. The seminar, organized by the East-West Cultural Learning Institute of the East-West Center in Honolulu and the Law Center of the University of the Philippines, focused on "Problems and Progress in Cultural Development in ASEAN", and the participants were asked to keep in mind the following passage in the 1976 Preamble to the ASEAN Treaty of Amity and Co-operation in Southeast Asia: "Conscious of the existing ties of history, geography, and culture which have bound the peoples together ...". Although the proceedings of the seminar have been published, I am grateful for being allowed to revise and enlarge my essay for separate publication. I thank Professor K.S. Sandhu, Director of the Institute of Southeast Asian Studies, for accepting the revised version.

I have taught earlier Southeast Asian history for a number of years and I have chosen to chart my course through different parts of the region at particular times rather than try to demonstrate that "Southeast Asia" possesses some predestined regional and historical identity which is disclosing itself over the centuries. My approach probably began as a reaction against the general assumption when I entered the field that earlier Southeast Asia could be studied from the perspective of "Indianized states". More than enough evidence seemed available to indicate widespread Indian cultural influences, and this circumstance undoubtedly encouraged scholars to see the region as having a historical identity of its own. India-ward proclivities never satisfied me, and I increasingly eschewed efforts to organize my lectures around overarching regional-scale themes. Instead, I concentrated my attention on subregional histories wherever the materials made this possible. Thus, the Manila seminar, with its focus on ASEAN, gave me an unexpected opportunity to ask myself whether Southeast Asia was indeed something more than just a geographical space between India and China. I began to enquire whether a regional history could be distinguished in the shape of cultural communalities and intra-regional relationships.

The reader will decide whether my sudden change of approach has made a great deal of difference to my perception of Southeast Asia as a zone of subregional histories. For my part, the experience of writing this paper has convinced me of the acute problems that would arise if I were to attempt to write a textbook on the subject. Fernand Braudel, the historian of the Mediterranean in the sixteenth century, refers to the "still unresolved debate" on the question of dividing history "into the slow- and fast-moving levels, structure and conjuncture".[1] How much more serious is the historian's predicament in my field, where a wide range of happenings is seldom disclosed anywhere, while the intellectual, social, economic, and political structures within which events at different times took place are still indistinct unless one seeks refuge, for instance, in the phantom of the *devarāja* or other generalizations supposed to do justice to this share of the world's earlier history.

Some may disagree that the difficulty of organizing an outline for a new textbook means that the enterprise should be shelved for the time being. Yet those who study and teach earlier Southeast Asian history may wish, once in their lifetime, to indicate the type of textbook that could take into account some of the themes and subject matter which seem, in our present state of knowledge, to endow the field with an appropriate shape and texture. This publication is not intended to be a miniature textbook but rather a gesture on these lines, and I hope that it may generate discussion of what is meant by earlier Southeast Asian history and the ways in which the subject could be presented.

In the meantime, the most helpful general surveys for me are D.G.E. Hall's *A History of South-East Asia,* first published in 1955 when the author had the responsibility of teaching undergraduates,[2] and George Coedès's *The Indianized States of Southeast Asia*, a critical manual of current research, originally written in 1944 and revised under new titles in 1948, 1964, and 1968.[3] Perhaps a serviceable new textbook could be written by someone willing to prepare a careful

1. Fernand Braudel, *The Mediterranean and the Mediterranean World in the Age of Philip II*, vol. 2, p. 1242.
2. The fourth edition has been published in 1981 by St. Martin's Press, New York. Hall's life (1891–1979) and career are described in C.D. Cowan, *Southeast Asian History and Historiography. Essays presented to D.G.E. Hall*, pp. 11–23.
3. The 1964 French edition has been translated, with some additional materials, as *The Indianized States of Southeast Asia* (Honolulu: East-West Center Press,

commentary, with ample footnotes and within Coedès's format, which could indicate new materials or revisionary views which Coedès was unable to consider before he died in 1969.

I offer this publication for classroom criticism. Teachers and students may soon detect errors, compromises, inconsistencies, and hesitance when I lurch in this or that direction in search of a shape to earlier Southeast Asian history. Not all may be interested in following the path outlined in chapter five where I discuss a particular manifestation of historical processes. Nevertheless, exploring processes rather than devising ways of stating the finished product of history in this region makes the field, in my opinion, exciting as well as difficult. I regret that I have provided too few suggestions concerning the important topic of continuities and changes, while my recourse to a synoptic approach saps the subject of its life and authenticity. Though I move beyond the fifteenth century when it serves my purpose to do so, my focus is on the earlier centuries. My neglect of Theravāda Buddhism, Islam, and Western involvement deprives me of opportunities for delineating the subject more sharply, but I believe that the time span I have chosen has a privileged status in the region's history. In the sixteenth century, the Portuguese reached Southeast Asia, and the Spaniards, Dutch, and English followed them within the next hundred years. I do not for one moment assume that almost immediately afterwards sudden and overwhelming changes got under way, but gradually parts of the region and also of the Asian maritime world in general, to which Southeast Asia had so profitably belonged, were no longer left entirely to themselves. The situation had been very different during the previous millennium and more, when what I shall refer to as the early Southeast Asian political systems elaborated their own style of intra-regional relations.

Some critics will bring their special disciplinary competence into play and enquire whether I could have developed alternative and more accurate perspectives. I would welcome this criticism most of all. Over the years my conviction has grown that the study of earlier Southeast Asian history is everyone's business. Not only historians but also anthropologists, art historians, linguists, and musicologists, to mention some obvious examples, must continue to make their contribution by showing ways in which the subject can be profitably studied. Only then will a more substantial rendering of the shape of regional history be gradually disclosed.

1968). For Coedès's life (1886–1969) and career, see J. Filliozat, "Notice sur la vie et les travaux de M. George Coedès", *Bulletin de l'École Française d'Extrême-Orient* 57 (1970): 1–24.

One way of defining the historian's responsibility, at least in respect of the earlier centuries, may well be learning how to study his subject. His colleagues in other disciplines can sometimes come to his assistance. The historian almost invariably finds himself asking what exactly he is looking at when confronted by a piece of evidence or, when he reads a published study, what its wider implications could be in a field where much is still obscure. Harry Benda, the first director of the Institute of Southeast Asian Studies, saw the future as one of inter-disciplinary co-operation when he argued the case for a "structural approach" to Southeast Asian history and proceeded to experiment with the tools of the social sciences.[4] Uncertain whether an ancient regional infrastructure had as yet been established, he preferred to examine the structure of Southeast Asian history in the social, economic, and political relationships of the "classical period" and especially in more recent centuries.

I must hasten to add, however, that, although I gladly recognize the contribution of those who do not normally identify themselves as professional historians, I do not mean to imply that the historians' skills stem simply from the circumstance that they, and only they, can be expected to assume the responsibility of discovering and criticizing documents. Mary Wright, Harry Benda's colleague at Yale, wrote an essay which cowed historians can read to their advantage. She points out that social scientists and others "are dependent on historians to open up general ranges of [Chinese] experience as it is recorded before they can define important problems in their own field", and she goes on to insist that the historians' function should not be defined as "doing the dirty work with the sources and asking social scientists to do the thinking".[5] I shall have occasion later to return to Mary Wright's defence of my profession.

I am grateful to friends for criticism of earlier drafts of this essay, particularly James A. Boon, Sunait Chutintaranond, Jonathan Culler, John M. Echols, Shelly Errington, Edward W. Fox, George McT. Kahin, Steven L. Kaplan, A. Thomas Kirsch, Stanley J. O'Connor, Craig J. Reynolds, and Harold Shadick. Not all of them read entire drafts, and none of them should be held responsible for

4. H.J. Benda, "The Structure of Southeast Asian History", *Journal of Southeast Asian History* 3, no. 1 (1962): 106–38. Benda's scholarly contributions, cut short by his untimely death in 1971, are described by George McT. Kahin, "In Memoriam: Harry J. Benda", *Indonesia* 13 (1972): 211–12; and Ruth T. McVey, *Southeast Asian Transitions. Approaches through Social History*, pp. 4–5.
5. Mary C. Wright, "Chinese History and the Historical Vocation", *Journal of Asian Studies* (*JAS*) 23, no. 4 (1964): 515.

what I have written. I also wish to thank Teresa M. Palmer for her typing assistance and for her patience.

The essay begins with some comments on what I believe are features of the cultural background from which the early political systems emerged. I shall then review the style of intra-regional relations which developed during the first millennium or so of the Christian era and begin to ask myself what we may mean by "Southeast Asian history". Thereafter I go my own way but not, I hope, into the wilderness.

CHAPTER ONE

Some Features of the Cultural Matrix

A remarkable development in Southeast Asian studies since the Second World War has been the steadily improving knowledge of the region's prehistory.[1] The best known discoveries, made possible by scientifically conducted excavations and the tools of carbon dating, thermoluminescence, and palaeobotany, are signs of bronze-working and domesticated agriculture at certain sites in northeastern Thailand attributable to the fourth millennium BC. Iron-working, too, seems to have been under way at one of these sites by about 1500 BC. Moreover, by the second half of the second millennium BC at the latest, metallurgy had become the most recent stage in a local cultural process over a sufficiently wide area in northern Vietnam to permit Vietnamese archaeologists to broach sophisticated sociological enquiries.

For my purpose, the important consequence of current prehistoric research is that an outline of the ancient settlement map is beginning to be disclosed. The map seems to comprise numerous networks of relatively isolated but continuously occupied dwelling sites, where residential stability was achieved by exploiting local environmental

1. For recent surveys of current prehistoric research, see I.W. Mabbett, "The 'Indianization' of Southeast Asia: Reflections on Prehistoric Sources", *Journal of Southeast Asian Studies* (hereafter cited as *JSEAS*) 8, no. 1 (1977): 1–14; the "Introduction" in R.B. Smith and W. Watson, eds., *Early South East Asia. Essays in Archaeology, History and Historical Geography* (hereafter cited as *Early South East Asia*), pp. 3–14; Donn Bayard, "The Roots of Indochinese Civilisation", *Pacific Affairs* 51, no. 1 (1980): 89–114; Nguyễn Phuc Long, "Les nouvelles recherches archéologiques au Vietnam ...", *Arts Asiatiques,* Numéro special, 31 (1975); Jeremy H.C.S. Davidson, "Archaeology in Northern Viet-Nam since 1954", in *Early South East Asia*, pp. 98–124; and Hà Văn Tân, "Nouvelles recherches préhistoriques et protohistoriques au Vietnam", *Bulletin de l'École Francaise d'Extrême-Orient* (hereafter cited as *BEFEO*) 68 (1980): 113–54.

resources to sustain what is sometimes called continually expanding "broad spectrum" subsistence economies. The inhabitants' original skills were those of "forest efficiency", or horticulture, although during the second millennium BC domesticated modes of wet-rice agriculture were probably appearing in the mainland alluvial plains.[2]

These tendencies in prehistoric research provide helpful perspectives for historians of the early Southeast Asian political systems, for they are now being encouraged to suppose that by the beginning of the Christian era a patchwork of small settlement networks of great antiquity stretched across the map of Southeast Asia. For example, no less than about three hundred settlements, datable by their artifacts as belonging to the seventh and eighth centuries AD, have been identified in Thailand alone by means of aerial photography.[3] Seen from the air, they remind one of craters scattered across the moon's surface. The seventh-century inscriptions of Cambodia mention as many as thirteen toponyms sufficiently prominent to be known by Sanskritic names. The multiplicity of Khmer centres, for there were surely more than thirteen, contradicts the impression provided by Chinese records of protohistoric Cambodia that there was only a single and enduring "kingdom of Funan".[4] "Funan" should not, I shall suggest below, be invoked as the earliest model of an "Indianized state" in Southeast Asia.

The historian, studying the dawn of recorded Southeast Asian history, can now suppose with reasonable confidence that the region was demographically fragmented. The ethnic identity and remotest origins of these peoples are questions that I shall eschew. Before the Second World War, prehistorians framed hypotheses based on tool typology to argue that culturally significant migrations into the region took place from the second half of the second millennium BC. These hypotheses have now been overtaken by the disclosing chronology of much earlier technological innovation established by means of prehistoric archaeology. Rather than assuming migrations from outside the region, we can be guided by Donn Bayard's view that prehistoric Southeast Asia was a "continually shifting mosaic of small

2. See Donn Bayard, op. cit., p. 105, for an evaluation of the evidence of rice-cultivation techniques.
3. I am grateful to Srisakra Vallibhotama for this information.
4. Claude Jacques, "'Funan'. 'Zhenla.' The Reality concealed by these Chinese Views of Indochina", in *Early South East Asia*, p. 378; O.W. Wolters, "North-western Cambodia in the seventh century", *Bulletin of the School of Oriental and African Studies* (hereafter cited as *BSOAS*) 37, no. 2 (1974): 378–79; and "Khmer 'Hinduism' in the Seventh Century", in *Early South East Asia*, p. 429.

cultural groups, resembling in its complexity the distribution of the modern hill tribes".[5] The focus of attention must be on what some of these groups could do inside the region and what they became.

The ancient inhabitants of Southeast Asia were living in fairly isolated groups, separated by thick forests, and would have had powerful attachments to their respective localities. I shall have occasion later to discuss the continuation of the prehistoric settlement pattern in historical times, and I shall content myself here by noting that in Java, for example, local scripts[6] and local sung poems[7] survived through the centuries. Or again, Malyāng, a small principality in north-western Cambodia during the seventh century, disappears from the records after the late eighth century but reappears in the late twelfth century as a rebellious area when Angkor was sacked by the Chams in 1177.[8] The modern names of villages and subregions are also often identifiable in early written records.

The multiplicity of settlement areas, each of which could go its own way, means that the historian should be cautious before he decides that any part of the region once occupied only a peripheral status in the general picture. Everything depends on what the historian is looking at in particular times in the past. For example, one still knows very little of the early history of the Philippines, but one should not conclude that these islands remained on the fringe of early Southeast Asia. Their inhabitants did not perceive their map in such a way. They are more likely to have looked outward to what is the Vietnamese coast today or to southern China for the more distant world that mattered to them. Every centre was a centre in its own right as far as its inhabitants were concerned, and it was surrounded by its own group of neighbours.

The ancient pattern of scattered and isolated settlements at the beginning of the Christian era would seem to suggest little prospect that the settlements would generate more extensive contact between

---

5. Donn Bayard, op. cit., p. 92. Recent excavations at Ban Chiang in northeastern Thailand have suggested a movement of people into the alluvial plains in the millennium after the transition to wet-rice cultivation at Ban Chiang; ibid., p. 105.
6. J.G. de Casparis, *Indonesian Palaeography. A History of Writing in Indonesia from the beginning to c.* A.D. *1500*, p.72.
7. Martin F. Hatch, "Lagu, Laras, Layang. Rethinking melody in Javanese music", pp. 38–50. Old Javanese inscriptions show that those who called themselves "Mahārāja" retained the words "Raka of ..." in their titles to indicate their home territory; see F.H. van Naerssen, *The Economic and Administrative History of Early Indonesia*, pp. 46–55.
8. Wolters, "North-western Cambodia in the seventh century", p. 358.

themselves. The tempo of communication was probably slow even though linguists have been able to delineate major and overarching language families. The languages of the archipelago can be conveniently defined as belonging to the "Austronesian" language family. The language map of mainland Southeast Asia is much more complicated. In early times, the Mon-Khmer, or "Austroasiatic", family of languages stretched from Burma to northern Vietnam and southern China. The Tai and Burman languages were wedges thrust into the Mon-Khmer language zone. But the reality everywhere in Southeast Asia is likely to have been that the major language families were represented by numerous local and isolated speech variations. Only in later times did some variations take on the characteristics of neighbouring speeches, a development that gradually led to a more widely used standardized speech. Linguistic similarities were not in themselves cultural bridges. When, therefore, we enquire how these scattered settlements were able to reduce their isolation, we have to consider other cultural features with greater possibilities for creating more extensive relationships within the region.

There are, in fact, several such features, though we must bear in mind that not all societies can be attributed with identical features. Exceptions can always be found. Moreover, similar cultural features did not in themselves guarantee that extensive relationships would develop across localities as a matter of course, even if their inhabitants came to recognize that they had something in common.

One well-represented feature of social organization within the lowlands in the region today is what anthropologists refer to as "cognatic kinship", [9] and we can suppose that this feature was present throughout historical times. In simple terms, the expression means that descent is reckoned equally through males and females and that both males and females are able to enjoy equal inheritance

9. This generalization does not include important groups such as the Chams and Minangkabau. I am referring, for example, to the Burmans, Thai, Khmers, Malays, Javanese, and Tagalogs. I follow Keesing's definition of "cognatic" as meaning: (a) a mode of descent reckoning where all descendants of an apical ancestor/ancestress through any combinations of male or female links are included; (b) bilateral kinship, where kinship is traced to relations through both father and mother. See Roger M. Keesing, *Kin Groups and Social Structure*, chapter 6 and the glossary. Sometimes examples are found of nuclear families and neolocal residence. The *Sui-shu*, referring to Cambodia in about AD 600, states: "When a man's marriage ceremonies are completed, he takes a share of his parents' property and leaves them in order to live elsewhere". See O.W. Wolters, "Khmer 'Hinduism' ..." p. 430. Excavations in Bali indicate burials of nuclear families; see R.P. Soejono, "The Significance of the Excavation at Gilimanuk (Bali)", in *Early South East Asia*, p. 195.

rights.[10] The comparable status of the sexes in Southeast Asia may explain why an Indonesian art historian has noted the unisex appearance of gods and goddesses in Javanese iconography, whereas sexual differences are unambiguously portrayed in Indian iconography.[11]

A notable feature of cognatic kinship is the downgrading of the importance of lineage based on claims to status through descent from a particular male or female. This does not mean that early settlements were egalitarian societies; prehistoric graves with sumptuary goods and status symbols reveal hierarchical distinctions evolving from before the beginning of the Christian era. Moreover, the principle of cognatic kinship by no means implies that kinship ties are unimportant. The contrary is the case. Kinship ties are the idiom of social organization in the region and part of its history. For example, when the Khmers founded or endowed religious cult centres, their commemorative inscriptions mention a variety of male and female kinship relationships over several generations. Nevertheless, the forebears, members of the devotees' kin (*kula*), are not presented as a lineage. Certain forebears are signalled out for their personal accomplishments, but the focus of the inscriptions is always on those who are performing and commemorating their own acts of devotion. One inscription explicitly excludes the devotee's parents from enjoying the fruits of his devotion.[12]

The relative unimportance of lineage means that we have to look elsewhere for cultural factors which promote leadership and initiative beyond a particular locality, and I suggest that leadership in inter-personal relations was associated with what anthropologists sometimes refer to in other parts of the world as the phenomenon of "big men". Here is a cultural trait in early Southeast Asia that seems to offer a helpful perspective for understanding much of what lay behind intra-regional relations in later times.

10. The nuclear family was the typical family in the Lê legal code, and both husbands and wives enjoyed property rights; see Insun Yu, "Law and family in seventeenth and eighteenth century Vietnam". The Chinese census statistics in Vietnam during the early centuries of the Christian era purport to reveal an increase in the number of households rather than in the total population, and one would expect this evidence in a society practising bilateral kinship. I am grateful to Keith Taylor for the information.
11. I owe this observation to Satyawati Suleiman. For a discussion of female property rights and the appearance of women in negotiations with royal representatives, see J.G. de Casparis, "Pour une histoire sociale de l'ancienne Java principalement au Xème s", *Archipel* 21 (1981): 147.
12. A. Barth and A. Bergaigne, *Inscriptions sanscrites du Cambodge et Champa* (hereafter cited as *ISCC*), p. 20, v. 34.

The leadership of "big men", or, to use the term I prefer, "men of prowess", would depend on their being attributed with an abnormal amount of personal and innate "soul stuff", which explained and distinguished their performance from that of others in their generation and especially among their own kinsmen. In the Southeast Asian languages, the terms for "soul stuff" vary from society to society, and the belief is always associated with other beliefs. The distinctions between "soul stuff" and the associated beliefs are so precise and essential that they can be defined only in the language of each society.[13] Nevertheless, a person's spiritual identity and capacity for leadership were established when his fellows could recognize his superior endowment and knew that being close to him was to their advantage not only because his entourage could expect to enjoy material rewards but also, I believe, because their own spiritual substance, for everyone possessed it in some measure, would participate in his, thereby leading to *rapport* and personal satisfaction. We are dealing with the led as well as the leaders.

The consequence of what Thomas Kirsch has referred to in the context of the mainland hill tribes of Southeast Asia as "unequal souls"[14] was that men of prowess, after their death, could be reckoned among their settlements' Ancestors and be worshipped. Ancestors were always those who, when they were alive, protected and brought benefits to their people. Sometimes they were worshipped with menhirs, and a Javanese scholar has recently suggested that Javanese temples should be identified as the successors of the menhirs.[15] No special respect was paid to mere forebears in societies that practised cognatic kinship.[16] Ancestor status had to be earned.

13 Anthropological studies about "soul stuff" in a regional context do not seem available at the present time. Indeed, James Boon remarks in respect of Indonesia that "the ultimate comparativist accomplishment would be to plot the various soul-power terms — *semangat, roh*, and so on — against each other across Indonesian and Malay societies"; see James A. Boon, *The Anthropological Romance of Bali 1597–1972*, p. 240, n. 7. See Appendix A: Miscellaneous notes on "soul stuff" and "prowess".

14. Thomas A. Kirsch, *Feasting and Social Oscillation: Religion and Society in Upland Southeast Asia*, p. 15.

15. Soekmono, "Candi, fungsi dan pengertiannya. Le candi, sa fonction et sa conception", *BEFEO* 62 (1975): 455. Soekmono believes that the significance of menhirs should be understood in terms that apply equally to the "continental" Southeast Asian menhirs.

16. Francisco Colin, a missionary in the Philippines in the seventeenth century, provides an excellent account of what could happen to undistinguished sons of distinguished fathers: "the fact that they had honoured parents or relatives was of no avail to them ..."; see F. Landa Jocano, ed., *The Philippines at the Spanish Contact*, pp. 178–79. In Bali, where kinship is very important, the achievement of founding a line of descent is emphasized rather than that of perpetuating an

Sites associated with the Ancestors, such as mountains, supplied additional identity to the settlement areas.

Men of prowess in earlier times may sometimes have anticipated their future status as Ancestors. Pedro Chirino, a Spanish missionary of the early seventeenth century who was familiar with Tagalog society in the Philippines, tells us that those who had distinguished themselves would attribute their valour to divine forces and take care to select burial sites that would become centres for their worship as Ancestors.[17] This is the conceptual framework in which I am inclined to interpret the meaning of the much discussed *devarāja* cult inaugurated by the Cambodian ruler, Jayavarman II, on Mount Mahendra in 802. The cult, established by tantric procedures of initiation and only after a long series of triumphant campaigns in many parts of the country, assimilated the king's spiritual identity to Śiva as "the king of the gods", a definition of Śiva that matched the overlord status that the king had already achieved. To this extent, Jayavarman's *liṅga* cult, except for its unique name, could not have been different from the earlier rulers' personal *liṅga* cults, to which I shall refer below. But his cult, I believe, was also something else. He realized that his achievements had guaranteed his status as an Ancestor among all those Khmers who were connected with his kinship group, which was bound to be an extended one because it was organized in accordance with the principle of cognatic kinship. He therefore made arrangements, as the Sdok Kak Thom inscription of 1052 describes, for the perpetuation of the cult to enable future kings to invoke additional supernatural protection from their deified Ancestor. The consequence he had in mind was that Cambodia would always have a *cakravartin*, as he had become on Mount Mahendra. And, indeed, the kings continued during the tenth century to venerate the *devarāja* according to the rite established in 802; they did this even though each of them had his own personal cult.[18] Jayavarman's foresight can be likened to that of the Tagalog chiefs mentioned by Chirino.

What situation did the king foresee that would require the later kings to be protected by his cult? He would have assumed that, in the future, members of different branches of his extended kin would

---

old one; see James A. Boon, "The Progress of the Ancestors in a Balinese Temple-Group (pre–1906–1972)", *Journal of Asian Studies* (hereafter cited as *JAS*) 34 (1974): 24.

17. F. Landa Jocano, ed., op. cit., p. 142.

18. H. Kulke has shown that the *devarāja* cult must be distinguished from the personal cults of later Angkorian rulers. The cult declined in prominence after the tenth century; see Hermann Kulke, *The Devarāja Cult.*

sometimes struggle to seize the kingship, and he intended his Ancestral cult to provide a focal influence in preventing Cambodia from being permanently torn apart, depriving the country of a *cakravartin*. Feuds would be composed after the successful prince worshipped the Ancestral cult and thereby announced his claim to lead his kin in his generation and the right to appeal to their loyalty.

Sindok's cult may provide another instance of an efficacious Ancestral cult. Sindok was an eastern Javanese ruler in the tenth century. Erlangga, the conquering king of the eleventh century, worshipped at Sindok's shrine early in his career some years before he began his campaigns. Perhaps he was invoking additional divine protection and, at the same time, assuming the political initiative by identifying himself as the rising leader in his generation over all those who could claim descent from Sindok. In this way, he would have rallied distant kinsmen to his side in preparation for the adventures that lay ahead.[19]

The cultural phenomenon of "men of prowess" brings with it the possibility of mobilizing extended kinship ties within and outside a settlement or network of settlements. Those who had the highest expectations when they were attracted into a leader's personal entourage, whether as relatives or dependants, were those who believed that they, too, were capable of achievement. Characteristic regional attitudes towards "public life" would develop. Public life in a leader's service would become the only prestigious way of life for those who did not wish to remain anonymous. As the Bendahara of Malacca puts it, "work for the Raja" or "go and dwell in the forest, for shoots and leaves make a good enough meal for a man with a small appetite".[20] Public life would also be the stage for open competition for pre-eminence. Leaders and followers alike needed to validate their status by continuous achievement, and achievement often involved adventures into neighbouring settlement areas. As signs of a leader's favour, achievement and meritorious deeds were rewarded with titles and other gifts. The leader established hierarchy in the public life of his day, and one consequence was that many of the Southeast Asian languages developed special forms of speech for addresssing superiors. Finally, and very important in the extension of communications between networks of settlements, leaders in neighbouring areas would recognize the higher spiritual status of a man of outstanding prowess and seek to regularize their relations with him

19. W. Stöhr and P. Zoetmulder, *Les religions d' Indonésie*, p. 291.
20. "The Malay Annals", trans. C.C. Brown, *Journal of the Malayan Branch of the Royal Asiatic Society* (hereafter cited as *JMBRAS*) 25, no. 2–3 (1952): 119.

by means of alliances that acknowledged the inequality of the parties. In this way more distant areas would be brought into a closer relationship with one another.

Cognatic kinship, an indifference towards lineage descent, and a preoccupation with the present that came from the need to identify in one's own generation those with abnormal spiritual qualities are, in my opinion, three widely represented cultural features in many parts of early Southeast Asia. With this cultural background in mind, I shall now suggest a reification that lay behind a particular episode in the region's early historical experience and something that has attracted a great deal of attention for nearly a century.

I am referring to what is often called "the Indianization" of Southeast Asia. Rather than assuming that Indian influences introduced an entirely new chapter in the region's history, I prefer to see the operation of specific "Hindu" and therefore religious rather than political conceptions that brought ancient and persisting indigenous beliefs into sharper focus.[21]

The first inscriptions, usually in Sanskrit, show that there were numerous small territorial units, several of which a man of prowess could sometimes bring under his personal influence by attracting supporters and by developing alliances. But his overlordship did not necessarily survive his death. The earliest Southeast Asian polities, even when Sanskrit inscriptions were beginning to be written, were the personal and somewhat fragile achievements of men of prowess, and had not been transformed by institutional innovations in the direction of more centralized government. A polity still cohered only in the sense that it was the projection of an individual's prowess.

Into this cultural situation — for political systems are expressions of culture — Indian influence arrived, travelling in specific circum-

21. For a discussion of this question in a Khmer context, see O.W. Wolters, "Khmer 'Hinduism' in the seventh century", op. cit. The antiquity of the Southeast Asian connection with India may be greater than I have supposed. H.B. Sarkar has recently suggested that the *Niddesa*, a Buddhist text hitherto attributed to the second century AD, should be considered to be in existence not later than 247 BC, and that the Southeast Asian toponyms, such as Java and Suvaṇṇabhūmi, which appear in the *Niddesa*, were known to some Indians by that time; see H.B. Sarkar, "A Geographical Introduction to South-East Asia: The Indian Perspective", *Bijdragen tot de Taal-, Land- en Volkenkunde (BKI)* 137, no. 2–3 (1981): 297–302. Sarkar's suggestion will not surprise those prehistorians who envisage sailing by Austronesian-speaking people in the Bay of Bengal and the Indian Ocean in general from the second half of the second millennium BC; see Wilhelm G. Solheim II, "Reflections on the New Data of Southeast Asian Prehistory: Austronesian origin and consequence", *Asian Perspectives* 18, no. 2 (1975): 155–57.

stances which will probably remain unknown but which were certainly in the wake of expanding international trade in the first centuries of the Christian era. What is important to note is that, during these centuries when historical records begin to become available for a few parts of the region, the dominant impulse in Hindu religious beliefs was a "devotional" and personalized one (*bhakti*), organized around popular cults in honour of Śiva and Viṣṇu and also by means of élitist teacher-inspired sects whose members strenuously sought to participate in the grace of these great gods. The sects, the best known of which was the Pāsupatas, insisted that an individual could with personal effort, which would include ascetic practices and the pious cultivation of his faculties of volition and imagination, achieve under a *guru's* instruction a close relationship with the god of his affection. Hindu sectarianism is the religious influence which, in my opinion, explains why the ascetic ideal — an ideal that exemplifies heroic prowess — is emphasized in the earliest Southeast Asian inscriptions written in the names of chiefs and overlords, all of whom would have performed heroic warrior roles in intra-settlement relations.

I believe that Southeast Asian constructions of sectarian modes of Hindu devotionalism contributed in two ways to the development of Southeast Asian notions of political authority.

In the first place, a heightened perception of the overlord's superior prowess was now possible. The overlord's reputation for ascetic achievement, no matter how it was gained, could be seen as exemplifying the closest relationship with Śiva of anyone in his generation. Śiva was the patron of asceticism and the Hindu god most frequently mentioned in the early inscriptions. In seventh-century Cambodia, the effects of the close relationship was expressed in two ways. The overlord Jayavarman I was said to be a "portion" (*aṃśa*) of Śiva,[22] while Bhavavarman participated in Śiva's *śakti*, or divine energy, which enabled him to "seize the kingship".[23] Both references to kingly prowess are framed in language considered to provide appropriate Sanskrit equivalences of spiritual achievement.

The second consequence of Southeast Asian constructions of Hindu devotionalism has a close bearing on the pattern of intra-

22. As early as the seventh century Jayavarman I, a Cambodian overlord, was described as a "portion" of Śiva; see George Coedès, *Les Inscriptions du Cambodge.* (*IC*), vol. 1, p. 8, v. 3. Kulke also notes Angkorian references to kings as being "portions" of Śiva: see H. Kulke, *The Devarāja Cult,* pp. 29–36. For a ninth-century Javanese identification of a king as a "portion" of Śiva, see J.G. de Casparis, *Prasasti Indonesia II,* p. 272.

23. A. Barth and A. Bergaigne, *ISCC*, p. 69, v. 5.

regional relations in the succeeding centuries. Śiva was also the sovereign deity who created the universe. Thus, the overlord's close relationship with Śiva meant that he participated in Śiva's divine authority. His day-to-day exercise of power would have been constrained by the norms of his own society, but his spiritual authority was absolute because Śiva was its author. He participated in sovereign attributes of cosmological proportions, and his supporters could come to realize that obedience to their leader was a gesture of homage that implied religious *rapport*, or *bhakti*. Their leader, a sovereign, partook of divinity and could therefore offer them the means of establishing their own relationship with divinity. "Kingship", signified by the personal Śiva cult of the man who had seized the overlordship and not by territorially-defined "kingdoms", was the reality that emerged from the "Hinduizing" process, but this does not mean that widely extending territorial relations were not possible. On the contrary, there need be no limit to a ruler's sovereign claims on earth. The chief's prowess was now coterminous with the divine authority pervading the universe, and this is how I interpret Jayavarman II's spectacular achievement and significance. He never tried to institutionalize the royal succession; the down-grading of lineage in the Southeast Asian cultures would have inhibited him from attempting to do so. On the other hand, his record of military success during a quarter of a century qualified him to institutionalize the contemporary criteria of leadership by proclaiming that he was a *cakravartin*. He formulated his status by means of his personal cult, the *devarāja* cult, and foresaw that he would be regarded as an Ancestor by his kinsmen. The criteria for kingship that he established were never upset during the Angkorian centuries.

A sudden reduction in the number of subregional centres was not the inevitable consequence of divine kingship, but more sustained efforts could be made to bring relatively distant subregions under the influence of particular men of prowess.[24]

This sketch of the "Hinduizing" process is only one approach to the subject of Southeast Asian protohistory, but it may be closer to the realities behind the early political systems of the region than if the point of departure is the establishment of "Indianized states", with the assumption that a state should exhibit certain recognizable characteristics. Protohistoric change, as I interpret it, took the guise

---

24. In seventh-century Cambodia, the overlord Jayavarman I seems to have recognized the obligation of bringing northwestern Cambodia under his influence in order to make good his claim to overlord status; see Wolters, "Northwestern Cambodia ...", pp. 383–84.

of heightened self-perceptions by the chieftain class in general rather than of far-reaching institutional changes in the status of a particular chief in a specific subregion, who now became a *rāja*. We need not imagine an almost conspiratorial manipulation of foreign ideas for promoting the interests of a few enterprising chiefs who were beginning to realize that their material resources were in world-wide demand, with the result of the conspiracy being that the royal beneficiary of "Indianization" was able to get permanently outside and above his own society and move closer to the gods who "legitimatized" his new status.

Difficulties are bound to arise in studying continuities in early Southeast Asian experiences when one thinks of "states", as I have done for too long.[25] Even prehistorians, when they are correcting earlier misapprehensions about what happened during the several millennia before the beginning of the Christian era, may tend to reinforce earlier dogma about the appearance of "states" during protohistory. Prehistorians are interested in "incipient state formation and political centralization" prior to Indian influence, but, while they can now show that Indian influence did not move into a vacuum when it brought a "state" like Funan into being,[26] they still cannot rid themselves of an awareness of discontinuity between prehistory and protohistory. The reason is that they take "Funan" as their model of the first fully-fledged state and attribute to it such features as "the ruler's strategy of monumental self-validation" and "time-tested Indian strategies of temple-founding, inscription-raising, and support for brahmanical royal cults".[27] A state, according to this line of thought which owes much to Van Leur's ideas in the 1930s, must be distinguished from anything else in prehistory. The effect is that a new lease of life is given to the significance of Indian influence.

I suggest that a gap persists between prehistory and protohistory represented by "Funan" because different terminologies are used

25. Virginia Matheson, writing about the inhabitants of the Riau-Lingga archipelago as they are described in the *Tuhfat al-Nafis*, addresses this matter of terminology: "... I can find in the *Tuhfat* no evidence for the existence of the state as a concept, an abstract ideal above and beyond the ruler, which was to be sustained and protected. What does seem to have existed was a complex system of personal loyalties, which it was in the ruler's interest to maintain": see Virginia Matheson, "Concepts of state in the *Tuhfat al-Nafis* [The Precious Gift]" in *Pre-Colonial State Systems in Southeast Asia*, p. 21.

26. Donn Bayard, op. cit., p. 106.

27. Bennet Bronson, "The Late Prehistory and Early History of Central Thailand with special reference to Chansen," in *Early South East Asia*, p. 316.

when discussing each period. An outline of "incipient state formation" depends on such Western terms as "fairly extensive trade relations", wet-rice, iron technology, and "probably increasing population density and political centralization in some of the alluvial plains of the mainland".[28] These terms, taken by themselves, signify economic developments that would be accompanied by the appearance of more complex political systems. Nevertheless, prehistorians have to deny prehistory the achievement of "statehood" by indigenous processes because of what they believe is known of the fully-fledged "state of Funan". The elaboration of the features of a "Funanese" typology, however, depends on an altogether different set of signifiers that owe their origin to Chinese documents and are therefore influenced by Chinese preconceptions of a "state". The Chinese supposed, for example, that any state should be associated with rules of dynastic succession and be described by fixed boundaries. No such polity existed anywhere in earlier Southeast Asian history except, as we shall see below, in Vietnam. Yet the Chinese were unable to conceptualize "Funan" as being anything other than a "state", albeit an unstable one, and, because of this Chinese perspective, "Funan" has become the earliest Southeast Asian example of what sociologists refer to as a "patrimonial bureaucracy", a model that does not seem to fit the prehistoric evidence.[29]

The two sets of signifiers — Western and Chinese — have precise meaning only in cultural contexts outside Southeast Asia, and the result of linguistic confusion is that the passage of the region from prehistory to protohistory reads in language that is bound to give the impression that the Southeast Asian peoples could graduate to statehood only with the assistance of Indian influence. The same reading may even lead scholars to postulate a lag in the process of state formation in some parts of the region, exemplified by the "impermanence" of certain polities,[30] or to assume that particular

28. Donn Bayard, op. cit., p. 106.

29. Ibid., p. 107. Karl Hutterer, studying how far the lowland societies of the Philippines had reached urban and state formation on the eve of the Spanish intervention, observes that "there is no evidence whatsoever for the formation of bureaucratic structure that would have been interjected between the chief and the daily affairs of politics, commerce and religion, as is usually found in state societies"; see Karl L. Hutterer, "Prehistoric Trade and the Evolution of Philippine Societies: a Reconsideration", *Economic and Social Interaction in Southeast Asia: Perspectives from Prehistory, History, and Ethnology*, p. 191.

30. See for example, B. Bronson, "Exchange at the Upstream and Downstream Ends: Notes Toward a Functional Model of the Coastal State in Southeast Asia", *Economic and Social Interaction in Southeast Asia*, p. 51; and Bennet Bronson and Jan Wisseman, "Palembang as Srivijaya: The lateness of early cities in southern Southeast Asia", *Asian Perspectives* 19, no. 2 (1978): 234.

geographical circumstances influenced the pace of the graduation to statehood.

In other words, the criteria for incipient and fully-fledged states are established by an arbitrary vocabulary drawn from an archaeology with an economic bias and from Chinese conventions transferred to a part of the world which was virtually unknown to them. The result is that one is in danger of looking for what could never be there in either prehistoric or protohistoric times. If, however, we think simply of "political systems" — a neutral expression — the way is open for considering other cultural phenomena such as religious and social behaviour that can be expected to affect political and economic activities in both prehistory and protohistory. No evidence at present exists for supposing that unprecedented religious and social changes were under way in the protohistoric period that sharply distinguish it from late prehistory. For example, there is no evidence to suppose that a chief's small-scale entourage in late prehistory was different in kind from the large-scale entourages of the historical period that supplied rulers with practical means of exercising political influence. In both periods, services are likely to have been rewarded with gifts of honour, posts of responsibility, and produce from the land.[31] All these gifts would be valued because the recipients knew that they participated in the donor's spiritual authority.

The territorial scale of a political system is certainly not the correct measurement for describing and defining it. Instead, we should think of sets of socially-definable loyalties that could be mobilized for common enterprises. This was the case in protohistoric times, and it would be surprising if these loyalties did not have their origin in prehistory. In late Balinese prehistory, for example, persons were buried according to their rank on earth,[32] which indicates some kind of hierarchy, with one person in the neighbourhood perceived as the point of reference for distinguishing ranks. This prehistoric background may be reflected in a Sanskrit inscription from western Java in the fifth or sixth century. The inscription has been translated as referring to a ruler's "allies",[33] but the term used is *bhakta* ("worshippers" or "princes devoted [to him]"). Khmer chiefs in the seventh

31. Van Naerssen suggests that the origin of the Javanese *raka* can be explained in ecological terms. The *raka* was responsible for the equitable distribution of water over a number of agrarian communities (*wanua*), and he therefore had the right to dispose of the produce and labour of his subjects; see F.H. van Naerssen, *The Economic and Administrative History of Early Indonesia*, pp. 37–38.
32. R.P. Soejono, op. cit., p. 198.
33. B. Ch. Chhabra, *Expansion of Indo-Aryan Culture*, p. 94.

century also frequently referred to themselves as *bhaktas* and venerated their overlord because of his spiritual relationship with Śiva which brought spiritual rewards to those who served him. The Javanese inscription may refer to a chief's entourage with "prehistoric" features but described in the Sanskrit language.

The peoples of protohistoric Southeast Asia retained, I suggest, much more than vestiges of earlier behaviour, though their behaviour would not have been identical in every locality. But their cultures are unlikely to be entirely illuminated by artifacts recovered from graves or by Chinese evidence of commercial exchanges in the protohistoric period. Tools and trade represent only fractions of a social system.

I have dwelt on definitions partly because I believe that the time is now promising for a re-examination of the passage of Southeast Asia from prehistory to protohistory in terms of continuities rather than of discontinuities. But I am especially anxious to indicate the origins of the early political systems that furnish the appropriate background to later tendencies in Southeast Asian intra-regional relations. I shall now glance at the style of intra-regional relations when evidence becomes more ample.

CHAPTER TWO

Historical Patterns in Intra-regional Relations

The infusion of kingship by divinity was bound to contradict the assumption that all rulers were equal. Each ruler was acclaimed in his own country as one who had unique claim to "universal" sovereignty, which was derived from a single and indivisible divine authority. The map of earlier Southeast Asia which evolved from the prehistoric networks of small settlements and reveals itself in historical records was a patchwork of often overlapping *maṇḍalas*, or "circles of kings". In each of these *maṇḍalas*, one king, identified with divine and "universal" authority, claimed personal hegemony over the other rulers in his *maṇḍala* who in theory were his obedient allies and vassals. Thus, a Khmer ruler in the early seventh century could be eulogised as "the glorious sovereign of three kings",[1] and the Angkorian ruler's polity in the tenth century could be rendered as "a pure circle of kings and brahmans".[2] The fourteenth-century Javanese poet Prapañca describes unambiguously the organization of space in earlier Southeast Asia:

> All illustrious Javanese Kings and Queens, the honoured ones who equally are distinguished by their towns (*nagara*), each having one for his own or her own,
> In one place, in Wilwa Tikta (Majapahit), they hold in their lap the honoured Prince-overlord.[3]

---

1. A. Barth and A. Bergaigne, *Inscriptions sancrites du Cambodge et Champa*, p. 46, v. 2. The Sung period transcription of *San-fo-ch'i* [Three Vijayas] for "Sriwijaya" may be an attempt by Chinese officials to give effect to a Malay envoy's statement that his ruler claimed to be the overlord of three areas, each of which was known as "Vijaya".
2. George Coedès, *Le Inscriptions du Cambodge* (hereafter cited as *IC*), vol. 1, p. 115, v. 71.
3. T.G.T. Pigeaud, *Java in the fourteenth century. A study of cultural history. The Nāgara-Kertāgama by Rakawi Prapañca of Majapahit, 1365 AD*, vol. 3, canto 6, stanza 4. A

In practice, the *maṇḍala* (a Sanskrit term used in Indian manuals of government) represented a particular and often unstable political situation in a vaguely definable geographical area without fixed boundaries and where smaller centres tended to look in all directions for security. *Maṇḍalas* would expand and contract in concertina-like fashion. Each one contained several tributary rulers, some of whom would repudiate their vassal status when the opportunity arose and try to build up their own networks of vassals. Only the *maṇḍala* overlord had the prerogative of receiving tribute-bearing envoys; he himself would despatch officials who represented his superior status.

Sometimes a *maṇḍala* would include no more than, for example, the districts in the island of Java,[4] but it could also be geographically extensive and contain peoples whose descendants today live in separate nation-states. The Malay rulers of Sriwijaya exercised some kind of authority in Sumatra and the Malay Peninsula from the seventh to at least the eleventh century. The Angkorian kings at intervals during the eleventh and twelfth centuries had similar authority in the Chao Phraya basin and the Malay Peninsula and also in parts of what is today southern Vietnam, and known in earlier times as Champa. The *maṇḍala* of the Thai state of Ayudhyā was, to some extent, the same *maṇḍala* which the Khmer rulers had once claimed to control but with its overlord in a new centre. The Javanese *maṇḍala* of Majapahit in the fourteenth century comprised Java, much of Sumatra, and no doubt parts of other Indonesian islands. Indeed, Prapañca claimed that his ruler "protected" most of mainland Southeast Asia. There is also evidence to suggest that similar *maṇḍalas* were in existence in the Philippines during the pre-Spanish period.

The *maṇḍala* organization of space was not, however, an invariably harsh reality in earlier Southeast Asia, though many wars have been recorded. One mitigating circumstance is that victories rarely, if ever, led to the permanent obliteration of local centres either by colonization or through the influence of centralized institutions of government. The *maṇḍala* perimeters continued to replicate court situations at the centre. Centres of spiritual authority and political power shifted endlessly. For these reasons, two skills of government

---

multiplicity of kings is also reflected in Mon tradition, where the term *smiṅ*, or "king", was not restricted to the ruler of Pegu. Shorto observes that no means seem to have been known in Pegu or Ava of extinguishing an extant kingdom; see H.L. Shorto, "A Mon genealogy of Kings: observations on the Nidāna Arambhakathā", in *Historians of South East Asia*, p. 69.

4. Pigeand, op. cit., vol. 3, *Ferry Charter*, p. 158 (*Yawadwipamandala*).

were emphasized and belonged to the tradition of public life in many parts of the region.

One skill was the gathering of what we would describe today as "political intelligence", or up-to-date information on what was happening on the fringe of a *maṇḍala*. This was of vital importance as threats could be anticipated. Thus, happenings on the *maṇḍala* fringes were as significant as those at the centres, and rulers who maintained communication with distant places were able to cultivate far-reaching geographical perspectives easily. In the early eleventh century, for example, the Angkorian ruler was in communication with the Tamil ruler in southern India and the Vietnamese ruler in Thăng-long. In 1592, the Thai ruler of Ayudhyā had surveyed the vast diplomatic space available to him when he proposed to the Chinese court an alliance to embarrass the Japanese prince who was attacking Korea in the face of Chinese armies sent to protect that country. The Thai ruler offered to invade Japan. [5] One of the Pahang Shahbandar's duties was to seek out information about what was happening in the outside world. The Shahbandar who was in charge of the port had contacts with foreign merchants and was well qualified to provide this kind of information.

The other governmental skill required of a successful *maṇḍala* overlord was one of diplomacy. He had to be able to dispossess his rivals of their claims to space in their own right, bring them under his personal influence, and accommodate them within a network of loyalties to himself, even though they often lived in distant areas. [6] Administrative power as distinct from sacral authority depended on the management of personal relationships, exercised through the royal prerogative of investiture. The same skill had been attributed to men of prowess in very early times when the scope for leadership was limited to small tracts of settlement areas, and it continued to be the source of governmental experience within a large *maṇḍala*. No clear distinction was made between the purpose and conduct of "internal" and "external" relations. In practice all relations tended to be perceived as personal and therefore internal ones.

In the situation I have just sketched, the ruler was not an autocrat; he was a mediator, accessible and able to keep the peace and mobilize

---

5. O.W. Wolters, "Ayudhyā and the Rearward Part of the World", *Journal of the Royal Asiatic Society*, parts 3 and 4 (1968): 166–78.
6. In the nineteenth century the journey by elephant from Battambang to Siem Reap took five days in the dry season; see Wolters, "North-western Cambodia in the seventh century", pp. 371–72. Garnier left Ubon on 10 January 1867, and reached Angkor nineteen days later; see Milton Osborne, *River Road to China. The Mekong River Expedition, 1866–73*, pp. 73–78.

many disparate groups. He needed to attract loyal subordinates to his entourage and to satisfy their self-esteem. One way of doing this was by organizing exciting court occasions at which the entourage was made to feel that it belonged to his company of faithful servants. This system is sometimes described as "patrimonial bureaucracy". The personal type of government, indicated by Weber's term, made a virtue of improvisation, and an illustration is provided by the Angkorian rulers' creation of special posts with ceremonial functions and prospects of future favours in order to attract particular sections of the élite to their side. [7] The rulers of the Angkorian *maṇḍala* had every reason to accommodate powerful kinship groups, each of which had its own network of relatives and dependants. Members of these groups could not easily be excluded from the royal entourage. They were normally invested with prestigious posts and shouldered administrative responsibilities; administrative power as distinct from divine authority had, to an important extent, to be shared. In Angkorian Cambodia, at any rate, large estates flourished in the countryside, and those who enjoyed the produce from the land were able to maintain their influence from generation to generation and to dispose of their customary land-use rights at will.

Ian Mabbett has suggested that "cliques, factions, personalities, clientage and patronage were essential elements in Angkorian politics", and I see no reason for supposing that this was not the case elsewhere in earlier Southeast Asia. [8] In Cambodia, womenfolk born into powerful families would marry kings, and their kinsfolk would enlarge their political influence as well as their rights to the use of land. The king's status was unique only because it was a religious one. In that sense alone he could confer but not receive, and his unique religious status helped to offset the disadvantages of the absence of a Chinese-style professional bureaucracy and of genuinely dynastic institutions that would identify the royal family and separate it permanently from all other families. Where lineage was not of importance in societies organized according to cognatic kinship,

---

7. I.W. Mabbett, "Varṇas in Angkor and the Indian Caste System", *Journal of Asian Studies* 36, no. 3 (1977): 429–42.
8. I.W. Mabbett, "Kingship in Angkor", *Journal of the Siam Society* 66, no. 2 (1978): 1–58, especially pp. 9, 13–27. Onghokham describes managerial skills necessary for regulating personal relationships in Java. The skills included mediating between higher and lower social levels and between the supernatural and men. A network of messengers and agents had to be deployed; see Onghokham, "The Inscrutable and the Paranoid: An investigation into the Sources of the Brotodiningrat Affair", in *Southeast Asian Transitions. Approaches through Social History*, pp. 113–19.

there could be no "royal family" in the strict sense of the term. There was only the ruler, and even he and his closest relatives would identify themselves with various kinship groups when the occasion required them to do so.[9]

Hierarchical structures were observed but informal personal relations and a highly pragmatic response to problems were not precluded. There was the minimum of bureaucratic procedures and the maximum amount of discussion, for consultation in societies knit together by webs of personal ties was bound to be a prominent feature of public life. Everything depended on man-to-man relations. Needless to say, the ruler had to be known to enjoy prestige in his home base if he wanted to exert influence in the peripheries. News of instability at the centre travelled quickly and reduced his outreach. One can even venture to suggest that a stable polity had to show signs of an ability to extend its influence further and further afield. A successful king needed wide space in which to flex his muscles.

The style of *maṇḍala* management meant that vassal rulers close to the capital as well as in distant places were treated with equal courtesy provided that they assisted the overlord in warfare and were not suspected of wanting to seek "protection" elsewhere. Moreover, the ruler often despatched travelling inspectors or agents to more distant subordinate centres in the *maṇḍala* to remind his vassals of his presence. Errands would include offering marriage alliances, building or endowing temples, examining disputes or complaints, collecting the royal dues, and echoing the splendour of the royal capital. Travelling officials, for whom rest-houses were sometimes reserved in the villages, were probably a major feature of government. A Javanese text defines an efficient chief minister as one who is "making the rounds".[10] The Angkorian *tamvrāc*, created after a tussle for the kingship, are a famous example of a special corps of trouble-shooters. The oath taken by these trouble-shooters in 1011 states: "If there is a matter of royal business on which His Majesty has ordered us to go

9. Cambodian genealogies were important not to justify a ruler's legitimacy but to distinguish those among his contemporaries — probably distant kinsfolk identifiable through their forebears — whom he could regard as his supporters. A genealogy would resemble the ruler's order of battle; see Thomas A. Kirsch, "Kinship. Genealogical Claims, and Societal Integration in Ancient Khmer Society: An Interpretation", *Southeast Asian History and Historiography*, pp. 190–202. For an example of an exceptionally dangerous Cham brother-in-law, see Coedès, *The Indianized States*, p. 165.

10. Pigeaud, op. cit., p. 120.

afar because he has heard that something has happened, we shall investigate the matter in detail".[11]

These are some of the expedients available to rulers in a region where geographical conditions and relatively small populations made for under-government. The sanction behind obedience was twofold. To serve the ruler was to earn spiritual merit,[12] but the ruler had also to have a reputation for being able to pounce ubiquitously and unexpectedly when trouble broke out. Strong government was, literally, on the move all the time. The sinews of government were the ruler's personal energy and surveillance. Yet, other and more palpably religious aspects of his authority were also important. The rites enacted in his capital and religious activity in the fields of art and literature provided additional signs that people were able to read as verification that government was in the hands of one who was destined to be a prince among men in his generation.

One particular religious aspect of the situation was that the rulers participated in Śiva's authority and therefore in the authority of the god who was also the *guru* of the universe. For this reason the rulers were expected to protect all cults and encourage spiritual zeal, and especially ascetic practices. The rulers were educative influences, teaching their people the meaning of spiritual well-being. The role of the ruler as a teacher, who originally interested himself in all modes of worship and attracted congregations of devout followers, may have lingered long in the region. The Bangkok rulers of the nineteenth century took an active part in mediating the acquisition of European scientific knowledge in Thailand.

I shall now glance at some of the famous *maṇḍalas* which adorn the textbooks on earlier Southeast Asian history. The *maṇḍalas* certainly increased the flow of communication within particular subregions and seem to mitigate the multicentric character of the region. Yet, the political influence of these *maṇḍalas* was rarely sustained for long periods of time, and it is difficult to indicate with precision the enduring cultural communalities that came in the wake of intervals of *maṇḍala* vigour. The communalities are as likely to have been the

11. George Coedès, *IC*, vol. 3, p. 209.

12. According to a Cambodian inscription, "kingship should be honoured by those who enjoy good works"; see G. Coedès, "La stele de Prasat Komnap", *BEFEO* 32, no. 1 (1932): 94, v. 27. The Prambanan and Sewu temples in central Java are surrounded by small shrines built by the rulers' loyal supporters. Sukarto draws attention to a Balinese temple with sixty-four stone seats for the ruler's brave followers, which are reminiscent of the megalithic Ancestral stone seats; see M.M. Sukarto K. Atmodjo, *The Charter of Kapal*, p. 9.

result of independent developments in centres which from time to time were under the influence of a *maṇḍala* overlord.

The Thai kingdom of Ayudhyā, founded in 1350, was close to Lopburi on the eastern side of the Chao Phraya basin, and Lopburi was at times part of the Angkorian *maṇḍala* in the eleventh and twelfth centuries. Scholars have observed how the Ayudhyā rulers assumed characteristics of Angkorian-style kingship. Yet these rulers did not bring all the other Thai rulers under their influence overnight. Although they were seeking to create a more centralized polity, a series of families occupied the throne, which means that there were frequent intervals of weakness in Ayudhyā.[13] Only in the nineteenth century was the Chakri family of Bangkok able to convert a somewhat loosely organized *maṇḍala* into a state where the component parts were much more responsive to the centre. Nevertheless, an important cultural influence brought a sense of communality among the scattered Thai centres in advance of institutional changes. From the thirteenth century onwards Thai princes were eagerly competing in seeking out famous Theravāda Buddhist monks and Pali texts in order to establish their centres at the forefront of Buddhist learning and piety. The unified Thai state at the end of the eighteenth century had long been a Buddhist country.

The Sriwijayan *maṇḍala*, existing from the seventh to at least the eleventh century, seems to have had more enduring cultural consequences, although the notorious uncertainty about its geographical span and political identity is a striking instance of the amorphous nature of the great *maṇḍalas* in earlier Southeast Asian history. Unanimous agreement has not yet been achieved on where its capital was at different times or on the extent of its hinterland influence. Not all would agree that, from at least the end of the seventh century into the eleventh, the capital was located near Bukit Seguntang in the Palembang region of southeastern Sumatra and only thereafter on the Batang Hari river further north, perhaps at Muara Jambi. One can, however, bear in mind that an Indonesian archaeological survey in June 1980 recovered from the northern and western slopes of Bukit Seguntang a sufficient quantity of green glazed stoneware, including true Yüeh-ware, unassociated with later Chinese ceramics, to es-

13. For an analysis of the Thai *maṇḍala*, see Lorraine Gesick, "Kingship and Political Integration in Traditional Siam", chapters 2 and 3. Skill in internal diplomacy was part of the Thai political tradition. No discussion of the *maṇḍala* system in earlier Southeast Asia is complete without referring to S.J. Tambiah, *World Conqueror and World Renouncer*, chapter 7. Tambiah sums up the *maṇḍala* system as "a hierarchy of central points continually subject to the dynamics of pulsation and changing spheres of influence"; see ibid., p. 113.

tablish beyond reasonable doubt that this area was in communication with China by the tenth century at the latest.[14] Perhaps the sherds are the remains of ritual vessels used in local Buddhist circles. To the best of my knowledge, no other site on the east coast of Sumatra has so far yielded Yüeh-ware on this scale. Inscriptions of the late seventh century and miscellaneous religious remains have already suggested that the Palembang area was connected with Sriwijaya. Moreover, a recent re-reading of a 682 inscription from the same area has revealed the toponym "Upang", the present-day name of a fishing village downstream from Palembang.[15]

Though a confident identification of Sriwijaya with Palembang is still premature, it is generally agreed that, in its heyday, Sriwijaya was one of the major emporia of Asia, through which regional produce reached the markets of western Asia, India, and China. The Sriwijayan rulers controlled the Malacca and Bangka straits. The need for a major emporium in western Indonesia diminished only when Chinese trading ships in the twelfth century began to visit distant overseas producing centres frequently, and the last records of Sriwijaya show that numerous coastal centres were thriving as if Sriwijaya had never existed. Changes that took place in earlier Southeast Asian history are not always readily discernible, but the appearance of Chinese shipping in the southern seas deserves to be reckoned as one index of change in the economic and political history of maritime Southeast Asia.

The Sriwijayan *maṇḍala* left a mark. From the Malay heartland on and behind the central and southern coast of eastern Sumatra, a Sriwijayan network of Malay-speaking centres developed throughout the Riau-Lingga archipelago of the so-called "sea gypsies" to the southern part of the Malay Peninsula. The process of Malay acculturation in this extensive area was probably assisted by the centripetal influence of the great Sriwijayan court, where services by the *datus*, attracted to it from outlying centres throughout the *maṇḍala*, took on the style of courtly hierarchy. The fifteenth century

14. The survey was organized by Satyawati Suleiman. For a discussion of Yüeh-ware found at Bukit Seguntang in 1978, see E. Edwards McKinnon, "Spur-marked Yüeh-Type Sherds at Bukit Seguntang", *Journal of the Malaysian Branch of the Royal Asiatic Society* (*JMBRAS*) 52, no. 2 (1979): 41–46. I am grateful to Pierre-Yves Manguin for informing me, in a letter dated 13 July 1981, that Feng Xian-ming, a ceramics expert in Beijing, has dated this Yüeh-ware precisely at the later T'ang period (618–905). The items were made in the Yuyao kilns of Zhejiang province.

15. Boechari, "Report on Research on Sriwijaya", *Seameo Project in Archaeology and Fine Arts. Final Report. Workshop on Research on Sriwijaya* (*SPAFA*), p. 5.

Sultans of Malacca were the heirs to much of this cultural tradition, and Malay royal traditions, expressed in the concept of loyalty and court organization, moved out to northern Borneo and the Philippines. This far-flung Malay political culture was reinforced by the profession of Islam, a widely circulating Malay-language literature, and frequent marriage relationships across the seas.

The conviction everywhere in this cultural zone was that busy harbours brought power and brilliance to the local ruler. In the western part of the zone, the determination to maintain such a harbour was fiercely defended when the Johore-Riau court, Malacca's successor, resisted the Portuguese and Dutch. The struggle for the Straits of Malacca ended only after the Napoleonic wars when the Treaty of London in 1824 artificially fractured the Malay world, but even in the second half of the nineteenth century the moral influence of the powerless Sultan of Lingga, recognized by Malays as the heir to the ancient Johore-Riau polity, was still to be reckoned with in the Pahang war on the Malay Peninsula.[16]

Early Spanish ethnographic rather than pre-Spanish written records assist us in conceptualizing the history of the Philippines in *maṇḍala* terms. Colin, writing in the early seventeenth century, states that in the past "there were no kings or rulers worthy of mention", but the model he had in mind was the king of Spain or the emperor of China. A more accurate perspective is supplied by his next observation: "there were many chiefs who dominated others less powerful".[17] He is alluding to the dynamic force in *maṇḍala* relations. The earliest recorded *maṇḍala* centre was in Mindoro island, southwest of Luzon, first mentioned in the second half of the tenth century as a trading centre known to the Chinese as *Ma-i* (Mait), whose ships visited Canton.[18] The disappearance of Chinese references to *Ma-i* in favour of Luzon may signify an important shift in Tagalog political centres on the eve of the Spanish arrival. But by then yet another *maṇḍala* was beginning to take shape, for the Spaniards arrived on the Luzon coast not long after this coast had become the extension of an Islamic *maṇḍala* based on Brunei in Borneo.

16. A.C. Milner, "The Malay Raja: a Study of Malay Political Culture in East Sumatra and the Malay Peninsula in the Early Nineteenth Century", chapter 5.
17. F. Landa Jocano, ed., *The Philippines at the Spanish Contact*, pp. 175–76.
18. For a recent affirmation of Mait's location in Mindoro, see Joseph Baumgartner, S.V.D., "Cotton — a Pre-Spanish Cebuano Industry. Facts and Problems", *Philippines Quarterly of Culture and Society* 3 (1975): 48. Father Antoon Postma, S.V.D., recently told me that he believed that Mait's likely location was at the extreme southeastern end of the island near the river Mait.

In the southern Philippines, Islam had reached Sulu and Mindanao more than half a century earlier. On all these coasts marriage alliances, always of importance in the construction of *maṇḍalas*, accompanied the advance of Islam. By about the middle of the sixteenth century the stage would have been set for a new and spirited chapter in *maṇḍala* history if the Spaniards had not occupied Manila. In the event, the surviving southern Muslim polities held their own, sometimes entering into relations with European "country traders" to thwart the monopolistic plans of other Europeans. The struggle for the survival of the Sulu Sultanate, with its foothold in Borneo and with fleets that swept the seas, ended only in the later nineteenth century when Spanish steampower came on the scene.

The early history of the Philippines reminds us of an essential feature of the *maṇḍala* phenomenon common in earlier Southeast Asia. The importance of a *maṇḍala* did not depend on its geographical size but on networks of loyalties that could be mobilized to provide armed power to leaders whom I described as "men of prowess". On the map, the Pulangi river basin in Mindanao does not resemble a large area, yet the rulers in this area were able to respond to Datu Uto's leadership so militantly that the Spaniards were kept at bay in the later nineteenth century.[19] Similarly, the mobilization of loyalties is the salient feature in the Angkorian political system, for example. The ability of such rulers as Jayavarman II and Sūryavarman II to wage apparently massive warfare contradicts the impression that they lacked authority merely because their executive power in day-to-day government does not seem to extend far beyond the functions of securing the material means for supporting themselves and their religious establishment in their capital or of being umpires amid a multitude of private and often powerful interests. Umpires are not captains.

See *South-East Asian Studies Newsletter* (Singapore, 3 April 1981), pp. 4–5 for news of a recent and proposed archaeological survey in the Pinamalayam and Mansalay areas of Mindoro. Mindoro was not the only important early trading area in the Philippines. A site occupied in the first and early second millennia has fairly recently been discovered at the estuary of the Agusan river in Mindanao, where a golden Tara image had also been found. The site is of unusual archaeological interest because the high water-table has preserved a considerable wealth of organic material, including a number of early boats. A wide range of ceramics has also been discovered, including highfired Chinese ceramics from the T'ang and Sung periods. Glass of Islamic origin has also been discovered. I am grateful to E. Edwards McKinnon for this information.

19. Nineteenth century history in the Pulangi river basin has been studied by Reynaldo C. Ileto, *Magindanao, 1860–1888: the career of Dato Uto of Buayan.*

The last *maṇḍala* that I shall mention is the Javanese one of fourteenth-century Majapahit. I have already alluded to the general circumstance that led to Sriwijaya's decline, which was the activities of Chinese merchants overseas. With the decline of Sriwijaya's emporium, Indonesian coastal polities outside Java were in no position to resist the Javanese ruler's claim to overlordship. Perhaps the claim was made to strengthen the ruler's prestige in Java itself. The island of Java was Majapahit's original *maṇḍala*, as it had been for Singasari, Majapahit's thirteenth-century predecessor. A scholar has recently suggested that even in Majapahit's heyday a potential Javanese rival existed.[20] We need not doubt, however, that Majapahit was greatly respected in the archipelago. Except in western Java and Bali, its style of overlordship was normally a relaxed one. Vassal rulers would offer tribute and seek investiture from the overlord, and some could expect punishment if they ignored him. *Maṇḍala* rulers coerced as well as wooed. The interesting question, however, is why these rulers should have been willing to acknowledge Majapahit's overlordship, and the reason may be another instance of the intra-regional associations which developed in earlier Southeast Asia with the minimum of force behind them.

One of the challenges awaiting historians, I believe, is the charting and evaluation of the extension of Javanese cultural influence outside the island. As far as Majapahit's influence is concerned, it can hardly be an accident that Majapahit was remembered in local chronicles outside Java rather than in Java.[21] Zoetmulder states that, in the middle of the fourteenth century, "Bali entered the orbit of Hindu-Javanism ... and in consequence Bali must be considered, from this time on, as belonging to the Hindu-Javanese cultural world".[22] Later I shall suggest that this impression needs to be qualified; the Balinese did not become Javanese. Nevertheless, Bali may have been more securely within the Javanese cultural *maṇḍala* than any other part of Indonesia. Other parts of the same *maṇḍala* should also be considered. In southern Kalimantan, elements of Javanese cultural influence have been identified in the *Hikajat Bandjar*.[23] Javanese court ceremonies were admired in southeastern Sumatra in the seventeenth century.[24] There are also references in Acehnese litera-

20. J. Noorduyn, "The Eastern Kings in Majapahit", *Bijdragen tot de Taal-, Land- en Volkenkunde* (hereafter cited as *BKI*) 131, no. 4 (1975): 479–87.
21. S. Supomo, "The Image of Majapahit in Later Javanese Indonesian Writing", in *Perceptions of the Past in Southeast Asia*, pp. 171–85.
22. P.J. Zoetmulder, *Kalangwan. A survey of Old Javanese literature*, p. 21.
23. J.J. Ras, *Hikajat Bandjar*.
24. B. Schrieke, *Indonesian Sociological Studies, part 1*, p. 57.

ture to sacral "Hindu" objects which, if not directly attributable to Javanese influence, bear comparison with similar objects in Javanese courts.[25]

My surmise is that Java in earlier times already had the reputation of being a treasure store of sacred learning. The purpose of the ninth-century pilgrimage by a high Cham official from what is today the central coast of Vietnam was "to acquire the magical science",[26] and the pilgrim's quest may epitomise Java's reputation for possessing esoteric knowledge. Central Javanese influence has been identified in Buddhist and Śaivite statuary and monumental art in southeastern Sumatra and as far afield in Sumatra as south Tapanuli. Javanese script has also been identified in southern Sumatran inscriptions of the tenth century. Panji tales may have been distributed abroad as wedding gifts to those who married Javanese princesses;[27] Panji tales are known in Thailand. Javanese shadow plays survive in Kelantan in Malaysia.

I have only mentioned a few examples of Javanese cultural influence beyond Java itself, and I have not attempted to discuss their significance. They serve to suggest that wider associations were possible even though the *maṇḍalas* themselves were, in comparison with the states of today, fragile polities.

My brief sketch of the *maṇḍalas* has not included examples from northern Thailand, Laos, and especially Burma. In every case, however, we are probably dealing with impermanent subregional associations which depended on the waxing and waning of particular *maṇḍala* centres and which never led to new and more enduring political systems. Cultural similarities may sometimes have been accentuated but not necessarily because of the *maṇḍalas*. Theravāda Buddhism flourished in several Thai centres but as the result of local initiatives. Sumatran and Peninsular courts survived the decline of Sriwijaya. Javanese cultural achievements could be respected outside Java, but the centres in the other islands continued to go their own way. The single exception to an otherwise ephemeral political scene is that part of the Angkorian *maṇḍala* which comprised the Khmer-speaking people. As early as AD 868, a centre in the Korat is described in an inscription as being "outside Kambudeśa",[28] and

25. L.F. Brakel, "State and statecraft in 17th century Aceh", in *Pre-Colonial State Systems in Southeast Asia*, pp. 56–66.
26. G. Coedès, *The Indianized States of Southeast Asia*, p. 123.
27. J.J. Ras, "The Panji Romance and W.H. Rassers' Analysis of its Theme", *BKI* 129, no. 4 (1973): 439–40.
28. George Coedès, *IC*, vol. 6, p. 85, v. 2.

the geographical precision suggests that by this time Cambodia could be seen from a distance as possessing some degree of territorial identity. The authenticity of the identity is verified by the fact that descendants of Jayavarman II's entourage were at that time enjoying land rights in northwestern as well as in southern Cambodia. The Khmer élite had a vested interest in the territorial integrity of metropolitan Cambodia and, by the end of the ninth century, Angkorian Cambodia was at the beginning of half a millennium of virtually intact survival.

Was the *maṇḍala* configuration of earlier Southeast Asia a divisive influence? I doubt it. Confrontations within and between the *maṇḍalas* are unlikely to have brought persisting prejudices in their wake comparable with those associated with the history of European nationalisms. Perhaps in the fourteenth and fifteenth centuries Burmans of the Irrawaddy felt that those who lived on their perimeters in the Shan hills to the east or the Mon-populated coastal plains to the south continually threatened them and were an affront to proud memories of the centuries when the Burman overlord lived in Pagan.[29] The reality behind the generally relaxed pattern of intra-regional relations in most of Southeast Asia becomes credible and vivid, however, when we glance at one part of the region where a different form of neighbourhood attitude developed.

In Vietnam, from at least as early as the eleventh century, the organization of territorial space was closely connected with the concept of a permanent centre at Thăng-long on the site of present-day Hanoi, from where action could be and was taken to eliminate other centres of Vietnamese power and to bind the countryside to the capital. The subregions of Vietnam became "provinces" and "prefectures", and the polity came to be seen as contained within mountainous borders preordained by Heaven and permanent in a manner that the porous borders of the *maṇḍalas* discussed above never assumed. The origin of this unusual geopolitical situation understandably owes much to the circumstance that, for a millennium, the Chinese emperors had persistently sought to enforce their authority over Vietnam and that, in the early eleventh century, the Lý rulers of re-independent Vietnam adapted the Chinese dynastic institution for their own purposes. The Lý initiative is another and important example of a fairly sudden change in one part of earlier Southeast Asia. Sons were able to succeed their fathers without succession disputes, and a linear sense of history took root. Borders became a

29. G.E. Harvey, *History of Burma*, p. 79. Harvey quotes an inscription of 1343. See also Paul J. Bennett, *Conference under the Tamarind Tree ...*, pp. 11–20.

dynastic trust and could never be surrendered without calling a dynasty's right to rule into question.[30]

This did not mean that the relationship between the Vietnamese centre and the countryside, at least before the fifteenth century, was as tight as it might have been in China when the dynasties were at the peak of their authority. On the contrary, Vietnamese historians, aware that archaeology is recovering the cradle of Vietnamese civilization long before the Chinese connection began, are alert to detect persisting folk conceptions of ruler-ruled relations. The historians are emphasizing a high degree of tolerance and the rulers' closeness to the people which affected the day-to-day conduct of affairs and which enabled the country to be mobilized in times of peril. Court customs were simple and informal.[31] Vietnamese historians are also investigating the Southeast Asian cultural matrix as a means of throwing further light on ancient Vietnamese society.[32] But we must remember that the Vietnamese, alone among the Southeast Asian peoples, had always to take China into account in their regional relations and not for the reason that the Chinese market brought opportunities for commercial prosperity as it did, for example, to the Mahārājas of Sriwijaya. Chinese claims to suzerainty, never abandoned, and unremitting Vietnamese resistance to the claims,

---

30. The founding of the Vietnamese dynastic system is discussed in Wolters, "Lê Văn Hu-u's Treatment of Lý Thần Tôn's reign (1127–1137)", *Southeast Asian History and Historiography*, pp. 203–26. De Casparis notes a further instance of institutional change in the form of the growing subordination of the Javanese village chiefs to the central government by the thirteenth and fourteenth centuries when compared with the situation in earlier times; see de Casparis, "Pour une histoire sociale de l'ancienne Java", p. 135. I have suggested that the frequent arrival of Chinese shipping in Southeast Asian waters should be reckoned as an index of economic change. An instance of ecological change is suggested by van Liere: "by the tenth century, the floodlands of the Mekong delta and the original settlements in the Mun-Chi basin were almost entirely abandoned". Perhaps there was a change in the flood pattern of the major streams; see W.J. van Liere, "Traditional water management in the lower Mekong basin", *World Archaeology* 11, no. 3 (1980): 271.

31. This statement is based on Trần Quốc Vu-ọ-ng's paper presented at the Eighth Conference of the International Association of Historians of Asia, held in Kuala Lumpur in August 1980.

32. See the essays in *Studies on History and Culture of Southeast Asia* (Hanoi: Institute for South East Asian Studies, Social Sciences Committee of Vietnam, 1980). Earning a good reputation in royal service was as important a feature of Vietnamese public life in the fourteenth century as it was elsewhere in Southeast Asia. For example, the Vietnamese annals state that in 1335 Doàn Nhu-Hài, a senior official, died rashly in battle because he wanted "to obtain very distinguished merit, surpassing that of his colleagues".

explain the Vietnamese stubbornly defended conviction that Vietnam and China, contrary to Chinese dogma, enjoyed comparable sovereignty.

This conviction was explicitly formulated as a repudiation of the Chinese claim to unique and central status in the world[33] and also as a Vietnamese restatement of the same claim in respect of Vietnam's immediate neighbours in Southeast Asia. The Vietnamese emperors came to perceive a difference between those who lived within their borders under more or less permanent administrative control and those who lived beyond Vietnam's western and southern borders. Dynastic memories were long, and the rulers gradually became convinced that to the west and south were "un-Vietnamese-like", and therefore unstable, political systems. This was, of course, a cultural judgment. Their neighbours seemed unstable only by Vietnamese standards of government. The reality in the other parts of Southeast Asia was that energetic rulers appeared from time to time, reinvigorated earlier *maṇḍalas*, and sometimes threatened the Vietnamese borders. Nevertheless, by the fourteenth century an uneasy Vietnamese attitude had crystallized towards the southern and western principalities immediately behind the mountains: they were regarded as a tangle of often disturbed lands.[34] The Vietnamese rulers were not, of course, beginning to arrogate to themselves a special role in the affairs of these countries. I am only describing the geopolitical situation as I believe they came to see it.

The Vietnamese view of neighbouring Southeast Asia can be distinguished from other earlier views of Southeast Asia as seen from within the region, where the rulers' limitless authority is expressed in terms of their personal and divine attributes. Claims to overlordship were always based on an individual's prowess and were not intended to prefigure a permanent extension of territorial influence. Rival rulers were often referred to as "evil" men because they were defying a divine overlord, and not because they were rulers of inveterately hostile populations. The view that royal authority was bound to be limitless is seen, for example, in the claim made on behalf of

33. Wolters, "Historians and Emperors in Vietnam and China: Comments arising out of Lê Văn Hu-u's History, Presented to the Trần court in 1272", in *Perceptions of the Past in Southeast Asia*, pp. 69–89.

34. See E. Gaspardone, "L'inscription du Ma-Nhai", *Bulletin de la Société des Études Indochinoises* 46, no. 1 (1971): 71–84. The inscription, dated 1336, lists several countries which submitted after the Vietnamese ruler's western campaign. The Vietnamese annals mention similar campaigns over the centuries in retaliation to raids across the borders. Sometimes the Vietnamese identified allied Khmer and Cham armies as their enemies.

Yaśovarman I of Angkor (889-910) that he ruled the lands from the Bay of Bengal to China. Jayavarman VII of Angkor (*c.* 1180-?) claimed that he received homage from the Vietnamese and Javanese. In the middle of the fourteenth century Prapañca, the author of the *Nāgarakĕrtāgama*, even included the whole of Southeast Asia, with the significant exception of Vietnam, as being under the protection of the Majapahit king; Vietnam is called *Yawana*, a Sanskrit word for "Greek" or "foreigner", and therefore, as the poet says, a friend. Those who wrote these records were conforming to the literary iconography of the attributes of divine kings, whose glory, sung by bards, would reach the ends of the world. Southeast Asian textbooks today do not have to disavow a distant past that menaces the present.[35]

I have now tried to distinguish some salient characteristics in earlier patterns of intra-regional relations. Exceptions will be found, but I hope that my sketch is not misleading. The *maṇḍalas* seem to provide a convenient framework for subregional histories, but they do not take us very far in identifying a shape to the history of the region as a whole. *Maṇḍala* history is a record of certain happenings inside the region and little more. The happenings were similar, and the reason, I believe, is that the political systems in question were no more than elaborated projections into history of some widespread cultural traits inherited from prehistory: cognatic systems of kinship, an indifference towards lineage descent, and therefore the significance attached to personal achievement in particular generations. These traits continued to be exemplified in many Southeast Asian societies but meant no more than that the élite's political behaviour in neighbouring areas would be predictable. This degree of communality of experience did not by itself lead to closer associations within an ever widening span of territory, even though the cultural influence of court centres would sometimes spill into neighbouring centres as part of the flow of communication in societies where monumental art, religious literature, and courtly style were valued. More needs to be known, however, before this kind of cultural outreach can be regarded as a long-term consequence of *maṇḍala* history. One thing is certain. The cultural influence of the *maṇḍalas* did not preserve them or reduce the multicentric shape of history in earlier Southeast Asia.

---

35. Little or nothing in earlier Southeast Asian history requires what Robert Schuman, one of "Europe"'s founding fathers, describes as the "désintoxication" of history textbooks; see Robert Schuman, *Pour l'Europe*, p. 49. Nothing prefigures a European-style contrast between a past that bristled with "national" rivalries and a present that is groping towards regional consensus.

Moreover, three general considerations should be borne in mind when one tries to ascribe a shape to the subject other than as the histories of numerous subregions.

In the first place, many people lived in distant highlands and were beyond the reach of the centres where records survive. The *maṇḍalas* were a phenomenon of the lowlands, and even there geographical conditions encouraged under-government. Paul Wheatley puts it well when he notes that "the Sanskrit tongue was chilled to silence at 500 metres". [36] One cannot assume that powerful overlords in the plains always ignored the natural resources and manpower in the hills and mountains, but the historian, relying on written records, has to remove vast territories from the historical map of earlier Southeast Asia.

Secondly, although there was an enduring multiplicity of centres, we have seen that the principle did not evolve that a ruler's sovereignty extended only over the territories under his influence. On the contrary, each ruler, an emanation of divinity, was likely to claim "universal" sovereignty. Thus, when the fourteenth century Javanese poet, Prapañca, supplies what may be a solitary vision of the whole region, he does so to eulogise the scale of his divine ruler's influence; only Vietnam is excluded from his magnificent *maṇḍala*. The centres he lists as "tributaries" or as being "protected" are probably compiled from commercial intelligence circulating in Majapahit's ports; the list is up-to-date because it includes Ayudhyā, founded only fifteen years earlier. No matter how relaxed intra-regional relations normally were, the paradox of a cluster of self-styled "unique" centres reduces the possibility that *maṇḍala* centres would accept each other on equal terms and gradually develop closer relations with each other. Far-reaching geographical perspectives probably came easily to the élite but did not permanently affect the geopolitical situation. Overlords, endowed with powerful personalities, required limitless space to leave their mark on their generation, but political space was rarely reorganized.

Thirdly, in the absence of linear history in earlier Southeast Asia, the conviction could not be sustained that the inhabitants of the region were moving through time into closer and therefore "Southeast Asian" relationships. Only the Vietnamese élite developed a linear sense of time, based on a sequence of recorded dynasties. The Theravāda Buddhist countries subscribed to the conception of linear history, beginning with the Buddha's birth and punctuated

---

36. Paul Wheatley, "Satyānṛta in Suvarṇadvīpa. From Reciprocity to Redistribution in Ancient Southeast Asia", in *Ancient Trade and Civilization*, p. 251.

by the Councils, but they were unlikely to have given up the notion of the centrality of their own country in the Buddhist world or the priority of the merit-earning present. People were aware of recurring cycles of good and bad government, but it was the present that always mattered.[37]

Such, then, are some possibilities and problems when one examines the proposition of "a history of earlier Southeast Asia". But an enquiry into the shape of the subject need not end here. Over the centuries other and not immediately obvious developments could have contributed to new experiences which were not only shared by many of the subregions but were also recognized by the élite as being common throughout much of the region. If this were so, history could have brought about consequences in the form of something recognizable as a "Southeast Asian mentality". The imprint of history could have been of greater significance in engendering a supra-*maṇḍala* and a self-conscious communality of outlook than could the independently held assumptions about political behaviour that stemmed from social and religious traits in prehistory and tended to keep the subregions apart. The historian can therefore enquire whether regional-scale themes, with intellectual implications, should be written into the shape of earlier Southeast Asian history.

My thoughts on the possibility of a thematic approach to the region's history have been stimulated by an essay written by Henri Brugmans in 1960 and published on the occasion of the tenth anniversary of the founding of the Collège d'Europe in Bruges.[38] Brugmans was the Collège's Rector and also a historian, and his essay is a comment on the movement towards "European" integration from a historian's perspective. He sought to organize a general shape to European history around the notion of an always developing common cultural heritage. I shall summarize what he wrote and then consider how far he provides a model for helping us to discern a similarly overarching shape to Southeast Asian history.

37. See Wang Gungwu's "Introduction" to *Perceptions of the Past in Southeast Asia*, pp. 1–8. The essays in the volume amply illustrate this point.

38. Henri Brugmans, "Un historien regarde l'intégration européenne", in *Sciences humaines et intégration européenne*, pp. 18–36.

CHAPTER THREE

Towards Defining Southeast Asian History

Brugmans suggests that a historian could be expected to view "Europeanising" tendencies with scepticism; Europe is the continent where "nations" and "nationalisms" proliferated. Indeed, the historian should be surprised that these tendencies have been accepted with such indifference. Brugmans suspects that the technical aspects of the economic issues at stake are too complex for the general public and that political passion has declined in the European countries after the Second World War; people realize that conflicts today are global ones.

Brugmans is careful to emphasize that the formation of the "Six" (the original members of the European Economic Community [EEC]) is a recent development and the result of special economic considerations. He insists that the "Six" do not represent a predestined *cercle de culture*. Even the geographical definition of what is meant by "Europe" has changed over the centuries. "Nothing," he says, "is more dangerous or more improper than to justify the present state of affairs by the *posteriori* historical argument. Nothing is more risky than to interpret the past as a function of present political justification".

Having uttered this warning, Brugmans pauses, for he has to acknowledge that those who identify themselves as "Europeans" have been influenced over the centuries by certain happenings: Christianity, the Renaissance, the Enlightenment, and nineteenth-century experimental science. The consequence is that European history is the history of "perpetual variations on a relatively restricted number of themes". To this extent, he permits himself to envisage a "community of civilization", by which he means the community's sciences, arts, philosophy, spiritual life, and social and political institutions, and he always gives attention to the historical variations on these themes brought about by ethnic diversity, geographical differences, spiritual roots, and languages. This, then, is the "Europe" whose major characteristics of communality can be readily identified from a distance. "However," he adds, "when we look at it close at hand, we are struck by the differences in time and space. Do these variations, then, contradict our affirmations of unity? In no way do they do so, for they are also part of the common heritage and can be explained only by that heritage."

Here is a measured, modestly conceived, and dispassionate definition of a common cultural heritage, where an interplay of shared cultural influences and local variations always exists. With this definition in mind, can we discern something that can be called "Southeast Asian history" in Brugmans' sense of an interplay of shared themes and thematic variations?

The sea provides an obvious geographical framework for discussing possibilities of region-wide historical themes. The sea facilitates communication between peoples, and there is much of it. Indeed, Coedès characterizes the Southeast Asian seas as "a veritable Mediterranean formed by the China Sea, the Gulf of Siam, and the Java Sea. This enclosed sea, in spite of its typhoons and reefs, has always been a unifying factor rather than an obstacle for the peoples along the rivers".[1] Coedès' impression of an enclosed sea has recently been reinforced by P. Manguin's demonstration that the reefs of the Paracels were avoided because of their navigational hazards, which means that ships had to keep close to the mainland coast when sailing to China.[2]

The peoples on and near the shores of the Southeast Asian seas were certainly in communication with each other from very early times. K'ang T'ai, a Chinese envoy sent to southern Cambodia by the Wu emperor on the Yangtze during the first half of the third century AD, heard of an emporium in western Java and knew that iron-laden ships were reaching southern Cambodia from an island out at sea.[3] A case has been made for supposing that the Javanese obtained gold from Kalimantan.[4] Again, Old-Javanese inscriptions mention mer-

1. Coedès, *The Indianized States of Southeast Asia*, pp. 3–4.
2. Pierre-Yves Manguin, "La traversée de la mer de Chine méridionale, des détroits à Canton, jusqu'au 17e siècle (La question des Iles Paracels)", in *Actes du XXIXe Congrès international des Orientalistes*, vol. 2, pp. 110–15.
3. I now believe that K'ang T'ai's *Ko-ying* should be reconstructed as "Kawang" in northwestern Java and is likely to correspond with the emporium known to Ptolemy as Argye; see O.W. Wolters, "Studying Śrīvijaya", *Journal of the Malaysian Branch of the Royal Asiatic Society* (hereafter cited as *JMBRAS*) 52, no. 2 (1979): 20. I now also believe that the iron-producing island of Tan-lan is more likely to be in western Sarawak than in the Philippines.
4. Brian E. Colless, "Were the Gold Mines of Ancient Java in Borneo?", *The Brunei Museum Journal* 3, no. 3 (1975): 146–57.

chants from mainland Southeast Asia.[5] Early Chinese records also refer to similar shipbuilding techniques which were practised in widely-separated parts of the region.[6] Manguin, the historian of Southeast Asian navigation, even suggests that shipwrights in southern China adapted features of the Southeast Asian ship.[7]

Maritime communications within the region did not, however, lead to permanent and substantial polities. The historical record, as we have seen, shows otherwise. The decline of Sriwijaya was accompanied by the revival of many independent coastal centres. Region-wide accessibility to the sea probably accentuated sub-regional tendencies by creating numerous and profitable landfalls. Chinese sailing itineraries from late Sung times plotted on the map some of the landfalls that were thriving on foreign and indigenous trade when the Chinese "tributary trade" fell into abeyance. Even the sea gypsies, the *orang laut* — a genuinely maritime population scattered over many of the shores and offshore islands of Southeast Asia — were absorbed into this or that *maṇḍala*, thus losing some of their original identity.

The contribution of the Southeast Asian seas was always to provide treasure for competing rulers, who even included some rulers living in an agrarian environment some distance from the coast.[8] Maritime treasure consisted of trade goods, harbour dues, and tributary presents from visiting merchants, which were made available to attract foreign merchants to the ruler's harbours, to embellish the royal centre, and to reward the ruler's entourage.[9] Maritime trade does

5. Jan Wisseman, "Markets and Trade in Pre-Majapahit Java", in *Economic and Social Interaction in Southeast Asia*, p. 211, note 13; and N.J. Krom, *Hindoe-Javaansche Geschiedenis*, pp. 264–65.
6. Pierre-Yves Manguin, "The Southeast Asian Ship. An Historical Approach", *Journal of Southeast Asian Studies* (*JSEAS*) 11, no. 2 (1980): 266–76. They used wooden dowels and not iron for fastening the planks of the hull, multiple sheathing for the hull, multiple masts, and two quarter-rudders. Outriggers did not sail on the open seas.
7. Ibid., p. 276.
8. I sometimes wonder whether too much attention is given to economic differences between coastal and inland polities in the archipelago. Inland polities, such as Majapahit, possessed sources of treasure in the rice-growing villages but were not so isolated from the sea that foreign trading revenue was not also available. See Satyawati Suleiman, "A few observations on the use of ceramics in Indonesia", *Aspek-aspek Archeologi Indonesia*, no. 7 (1980): 13, for a discussion of links between the central Javanese princes and harbour princes of the northern coast. The two types of polity should be compared in less narrowly defined cultural terms.
9. Milner, "The Malay Raja", chapter 3, analyses the function of trading wealth in a Malay court.

not seem to have stimulated the growth of an influential indigenous commercial class, with social status at home and regional-scale trading interests abroad. The tendency was otherwise. Rich merchants, often foreigners, aspired to rise in the local court hierarchies or were used by the rulers as an additional and reliable source of manpower for administrative functions.[10] The proceeds of maritime commerce helped, above all else, to enlarge the resources of the *maṇḍala* leaders, and the *Sejarah Melayu* pithily sums up the connection between the ruler and trading wealth in the words of Sultan Mahmud: "where there is sovereignty there is gold".[11]

When we compare the Southeast Asian seas with the Mediterranean, we should observe how Braudel perceives the Mediterranean in his classic account of it in the age of Philip II. Braudel suggests that the sea's unity was created by the movement of men over the sea routes. Movement certainly took place within the Southeast Asian "Mediterranean", but we should also remember the type of movement Braudel has in mind. He is thinking of the urban-based trading activities that predominated over all other activities. "Cities and their communications, communications and their cities have imposed a unified human construction on geographical space".[12] Or again, he says, "the history and civilization of the sea have been shaped by its towns".[13] But the Southeast Asian cities were not Venices or Genoas. They were royal centres, with trading ports under their shadow, where maritime treasure helped to sustain an *élan vital* that had little to do with commercial enterprise in our sense of the term. Correspondence going out of such centres would not have been in the form of enquiries about trading prospects but of missives with demands for tribute or even religious statues from

10. For Cambodia, see Kenneth Hall, "Khmer commercial development and foreign contacts under Sūryavarman I", *Journal of the Economic and Social History of the Orient* 18, no. 3 (1975): 321–22; for Champa, see Pierre-Yves Manguin, "Études cam. II. L'introduction de l'Islam au Campa", *BEFEO* 66 (1979): 260; for the Malay courts, see Barbara Andaya, "The Indian *saudagar raja* [the king's merchant] in traditional Malay courts", *JMBRAS* 51, no. 1 (1978): 13–35; for Java, see Jan Wisseman, op. cit., pp. 207–8. Pires refers to the way foreign traders aspired to princely style on the northern coast of Java; see A. Cortesão, ed., *The Suma Oriental of Tomé Pires*, vol. 1, pp. 182, 199–200. In Malay Malacca, some prominent Javanese merchants had links elsewhere in the archipelago but, by and large, there is little evidence of an indigenous commercial class with region-wide economic interests.

11. "The Malay Annals", *JMBRAS* 25, no. 2–3 (1952): 187.

12. Fernand Braudel, *The Mediterranean and the Mediterranean World in the Age of Philip II*, vol. 1, p. 277.

13. Ibid., p. 278.

overlord to vassal. Another difference between the two inland seas is that in Southeast Asia the arrival of foreign trading treasure could be taken for granted because some of the major ports were on the trans-Asian maritime route from western Asia to China. Merchants from western Asia, India, and eventually China frequently visited the Southeast Asian ports *en route* to other centres outside the region. The Mediterranean, on the other hand, was a terminus for Asian produce in the sense that the Mediterranean merchants cornered the produce in order to be able to redistribute it at a profit. Certainly, a brisk redistribution trade was plied in the Southeast Asian hinterland in addition to the collection of raw materials, but the trade included goods that never failed to reach the region from centres of production outside the region. Only Sriwijaya may have had monopolistic concerns similar to those in Venice or Genoa and only when its overlord was benefiting from the "tributary trade" with China before Chinese merchants themselves sailed to the southern seas in their own ships.

Thus, when we examine the sea's influence in shaping Southeast Asian history, we do not stumble on a helpful theme. The Southeast Asian seas fitted into the polycentric landscape.

On the other hand, the sea could also exert another kind of influence with possibilities for an intra-regional communality of historical experience. The sea to which I am now referring is not the Southeast Asian "Mediterranean" but what I shall describe as "the single ocean", the vast expanse of water from the coasts of eastern Africa and western Asia to the immensely long coastal line of the Indian subcontinent and on to China. The sea, defined in this manner, was, I believe, a significant fact of life in earlier Southeast Asia not only because treasure from distant places always arrived but also for other reasons that I shall consider. I shall therefore digress for a moment in order to discuss the reality that lay behind "the single ocean".

The historical reality is that, during the many centuries before the arrival of the Europeans, those who lived on its shores never had reason to suppose that maritime communications with the rest of Asia would be severed for long intervals by disturbed political conditions in any part of the single ocean. For example, changes outside Southeast Asia never affected the prosperity of the famous camphor-exporting coast of Barus in northwestern Sumatra; Arabs, Persians, Nestorian Christians, Tamils, and Jews all made their way there.[14]

14. Rumbi Mulia, *The Ancient Kingdom of Panai and the ruins of Padang Lawas* (*North Sumatra*), p. 3. For the reference to Jewish merchants, provided by S.D. Goitein, see Wolters, *The fall of Śrīvijaya in Malay history*, p. 208, note 34.

The single ocean possessed a genuine unity of its own. The trading connections that linked the opposite ends of maritime Asia resemble links in a chain which would join together again even if one link were temporarily broken. The fundamental unity of communications is amply verified in the quick recognition by the Portuguese at the beginning of the sixteenth century (1506-1512) that, in order to control the spice trade of eastern Indonesia, they had to erect a chain of fortresses from the Red Sea to the Moluccas before they could dominate the far-flung Asian emporia and monopolize the spice trade. Their ambitious geopolitical strategy never succeeded, and spices continued to reach the Mediterranean through Muslim traders. Coens, on behalf of the Dutch East India Company, proposed a similar strategy a century later when he recommended that his Directors should control the Indian textile trade to deprive Asian merchants of purchasing power when they sought Southeast Asian produce.

From time to time in the pre-European centuries a trading centre on the shores of the single ocean would temporarily seek to control two or more links in the chain. Sriwijaya seems to have done so in its heyday. Nevertheless, the seas remained open until the seventeenth century, and the Chinese imperial histories provide the evidence. The earliest Chinese records of the region in the first centuries of the Christian era disclose that the opposite ends of Asia were already in maritime communication with each other, and nothing happened in the next millennium to persuade the Chinese that the situation had drastically changed. The Chinese emperors, powerless on the high seas, were therefore glad to bestow marks of favour on their Southeast Asian "vassals" who had been attracted by the Son of Heaven's imperial virtu, were policing the seas on his behalf, and were keeping the trade routes to China open.

In effect, the single ocean was a vast zone of neutral water, which rulers inside and outside Southeast Asia independently and for their own interests wanted to protect. The Macassar ruler in 1615 was echoing the ancient experience of unimpeded access to the single ocean when he insisted that:

> God has made the earth and the seas, has divided the earth among mankind, and given the sea in common. It is a thing unheard of that anyone should be forbidden to sail the seas.[15]

Echoes of the same tradition reached Grotius when he wrote his *Mare Liberum*, published in 1609 to refute Portuguese monopolistic claims

15. Quoted by G.J. Resink, *Indonesia's History between the Myths*, p. 45.

in the single ocean. Grotius, aware of maritime practices in the eastern seas before the sixteenth century, wrote:

> The Arabians and the Chinese are at the present day still carrying on with the peoples of the East Indies in trading which has been uninterrupted for several centuries.[16]

The consequence of the freedom of the seas was a tradition of hospitality to foreign traders. All traders needed to be attracted by suitable port facilities, fair trading practices, and protection from sporadic piracy in local waters.[17] The maritime rulers of earlier Southeast Asia were always anxious to prevent lawlessness on the seas from diverting traders to alternative ports.[18] Piracy began to be a prominent historical feature in Southeast Asian history only when Raffles and his contemporaries were writing about the region, and the reason is that the withering of local economic power compelled seafaring peoples to eke out a living by violent means at the expense of the Europeans who had forced the local rulers to conclude restrictive trading treaties. In earlier times, piracy was chronic only in intervals between the fall of one important trading centre and the rise of another in the same neighbourhood.

The single ocean is a significant fact of Southeast Asian historical geography, and continuous and lively commercial exchanges can be expected to have encouraged cultural communications that left a mark on Southeast Asian history. "The Indianized states of Southeast Asia" have, in fact, long been a conventional definition in the region's historiography.

News of developments in India certainly reached Southeast Asia fairly promptly and continuously. We have seen that Hindu devotional cults, appearing in India in the first centuries of the Christian era, were making themselves felt in Southeast Asia during the same centuries. The great Hindu philosopher Śaṅkara (*c.*700-*c.*750) is mentioned in a ninth-century Cambodian inscription. Bosch was

---

16. I gratefully acknowledge R.P. Anand's paper on "Maritime Practices and Customs in Southeast Asia until AD 1600 and the Modern Law of the Sea", presented at the Manila seminar.
17. The Bendahara of Malacca epitomises this tradition. He was "exceeding just and humane, clever in his handling of foreigners and skilled in conciliating the goodwill of the populace" ("The Malay Annals", p. 134).
18. W.H. Scott substitutes "trade-raiding" for what the Spaniards called "piracy", and he observes that "what was reprehensible in Philippine morality was not the act of plunder itself, but doing it to those who had not done it to you"; see William Henry Scott, "Boat-building and seamanship in classic Philippine Society", pp. 26, 31. Scott's essay contains a thorough analysis of nautical and related vocabularies in the Filipino languages and is a marvellous example of linguistic study as a tool for cultural historians.

able to identify part of the Barabudur bas-relief as the "Gaṇḍavyūha", the last chapter of the *Avataṃsaka Sūtra*, a Mahāyāna Buddhist text; the *Sūtra* circulated widely in the Buddhist world to which Java and other parts of Southeast Asia belonged. Again, a version of a Persian Muslim epic reached Sumatra not very long after it was written.[19]

Prolonged and extensive communication over the single ocean brings the particular possibility of an Indian-influenced shape to Southeast Asian history. I have indicated my doubt that the shape would be found in the transformation of indigenous political systems, but this does not mean that we need not take into account one consequence when specimens of Indian literature, travelling as manuscripts or by oral transmission reached numerous centres in Southeast Asia. We can assume with some confidence that the élite in all these centres was gradually exposed to the epistemological assumption of Indian literature that statements in every branch of knowledge were valid everywhere in the world. The Indian manuals are organized to leave their readers in no doubt that their categorical statements had an incontrovertible claim to be the embodiment of universal principles.

Indian literature probably engendered a catholicity of outlook which should be assigned a place in the shape of Southeast Asian history. Because of the authority of the Indian manuals, standards of excellence would be recognized as universal ones, even if only few were expected to be able to exemplify them. And so the Javanese author of the fourteenth-century *Nāgarakĕrtāgama* claims that there are only two excellent countries in the world: Java and India. Their excellence is on account of the respect given to religious learning in each of these countries.[20]

But India did not always have the monopoly of books. Whether in the form of improved Sri Lankan editions of the Pali Canon of Theravāda Buddhism, Muslim modernism from the Middle East, or the teachings of Spenserian Darwinism in the late nineteenth and early twentieth centuries,[21] the Southeast Asian élite would, I believe, be alert to new possibilities for updating older statements of universal validity. I suggest that the élite always took modernity urbanely in its stride. An ancient preoccupation with the signs of the present, manifesting itself in an ability to hail genuine leaders in a

19. L.F. Brakel, *The Hikayat Muhammad Hanafiyyah*, pp. 54–57.
20. T.G.T. Pigeaud, *Java in the fourteenth century*, vol. 3, canto 83, stanza 2.
21. Akira Nagazumi, *The Dawn of Indonesian Nationalism. The Early Years of the Budi Utomo, 1908–1918*, p. 185, note 80; and David G. Marr, *Vietnamese Anticolonialism*, pp. 227–28.

particular generation in a particular area, would have contributed to a present-minded outlook which permitted the élite not only to expect the continuous flow of foreign merchandise but also to absorb the mondial perspectives of the continuously arriving Indian literature and sustain intellectually curious and outward-looking habits of mind for all time.[22]

We can go further and suppose that, in the different élitist centres, familiarity with the Indian assumption that knowledge was based on universal principles meant that there would be a disposition to identify something common everywhere in the region or, at least, to assume that something common was likely to be found everywhere. This habit of mind was encouraged by a special feature of the general categories of knowledge laid out in the Indian books. Lists of examples of a particular phenomenon would be provided, and at the end of the lists the word "etcetera" (*ādi*) would be written, thus enabling Southeast Asian scholars to incorporate further examples from their own experience. Indian literature could therefore be seen as providing models for organizing local subject matter.

This in fact happened.[23] Indian-devised expositions of universal phenomena left their mark. For example, the *Laws of Manu* state that "in the world eighteen points of litigation arise". A Majapahit law code modifies the substance of some of Manu's points to accommodate Javanese customary law but does not alter the number eighteen. Everywhere in the world of books the number had to be eighteen.[24] A Javanese manual on the science of poetics teaches the subject within the context of Javanese prosody, but its model is derived from an Indian manual on poetics that had fairly recently reached Java.[25] And in Vietnam, too, where there was familiarity with the Chinese as well as with the Indian world-view as reflected in Buddhist literature, a thirteenth-century historian used a Chinese

22. A very curious example of the updating of earlier conceptions is provided by a Burmese medium, who explained that the Lokapālas guarded the following four cardinal points: the Shan States, China, and Indo-china; India's holy sites; the Anglo-Saxons; and the Russians. See E. Michael Mendelson, "A Messianic Buddhist Association in Upper Burma", *Bulletin of the School of Oriental and African Studies* (*BSOAS*) 24, no. 3 (1961): 573.

23. For two examples of the use of *ādi*, see Pigeaud, op. cit., canto 9, stanza 1, line 4; and Mabbett, "Kingship in Angkor", p. 34: "In five days from today, I shall begin to dig ... (*ādi*)."

24. F.H. van Naerssen, "The Aṣṭādaśavyavahāra in Old Javanese", *Journel of the Greater India Society* 15 (1956): 111–32. "The eighteen points" were also acknowledged in Champa; see M.B. Hooker, *A Concise Legal History of South-East Asia*, p. 33.

25. C. Hooykaas, *The Old-Javanese Rāmāyaṇa*, vol. 65, no. 1.

format for writing imperial history as his model for presenting Vietnamese history, and several later Vietnamese historians followed his example.[26] Religious statuary provides an obvious instance of communality everywhere in Southeast Asia. In all parts of the region the élite was bound to be able to recognize the attributes of Śiva, Viṣṇu, and the Buddha, for the iconographic canons had been laid down as universal norms by the Indian scholars. Southeast Asian workshops supplied plenty of local artistic embellishments, but the distinguishing features of the statues were obligatory everywhere. And so the élite in different centres could perceive ubiquitous signs of its beliefs.

Here is a detail of an *aire de famille* in the nineteenth century. A Chinese trader domiciled in Thailand visited Bali. During his voyage he had prayed to the *tedja* of the Buddha, though he was probably thinking of his ruler in Bangkok. *Tedja* is a Sanskrit-derived word (*tejas*) often used to signify a Southeast Asian ruler's divinely radiant energy. When the trader reached Bali, the local ruler entertained him with ritual dancing, and what he saw was sufficiently familiar that he could compare the performance with what he had seen in Thailand and discuss differences with his Balinese host.[27]

Art, religion, and government are inseparable phenomena in earlier Southeast Asia, and we can broach a few more instances of what would seem to be a broadly based communality of outlook encouraged by the widespread circulation of Indian books. Indian books have much to say about "the science of government", and the Southeast Asian records reflect the same emphasis. Inscriptions tell us that Cambodian kings were "drunk in the ocean of the *śāstras*" or "versed in the science of politics". We find references to "the seven constituents of political organization" as they are laid down in Indian books. In all these instances we are dealing with material in Indian models that rarely made improbable demands on those who managed the Southeast Asian *maṇḍalas*. The Indian precepts frequently dealt with matters which would be common sense anywhere. For example, the need for consultation in Southeast Asian societies, knit together by many personal ties, was articulated in Indian works on politics by the injunction that rulers should consult their "ministers". Yet the fact that common-sense precepts were enshrined in

26. O.W. Wolters, "Historians and Emperors in Vietnam and China: Comments arising out of Lê Văn Hu-u's History, Presented to the Trần court in 1272" in *Perceptions of the Past in Southeast Asia*.

27. Elizabeth Graves and Charnvit Kaset-siri, "A Nineteenth-Century Siamese Account of Bali: with Introduction and Notes", *Indonesia* 7 (1969): 77–122.

writing that claimed universal validity would have enabled a Southeast Asian ruler to regard his own conduct as *comme il faut* and expect other rulers to behave in accordance with the same precepts.

The prestige of Indian models is reflected in miscellaneous records from many parts of the region. For example, a Cham king in the twelfth century supported his accession to the throne by writing a Sanskrit treatise which purported to resemble a *smṛti*, an Indian treatise with the status of a *sūtra* or *śāstra*.[28] He was issuing a statement which exhibited the aura of an Indian book on good government. Again, an inscription states that the Javanese king Erlangga in the eleventh century subverted his enemy's power "by the application of the means taught by" the author of the *Arthaśāstra*, the most famous of all Indian treatises on the policies of a successful *maṇḍala* manager.[29] The *Arthaśāstra* also contains many precepts useful for a would-be conqueror. It recommends that a conquering king should ally himself with the king whose territories lay at the rear of his own enemy. This axiom is common sense but, because it was mentioned in an illustrious source, it also had the stamp of universal authority. Whether or not he was consciously invoking the axiom, the Ayudhyā king in 1592 was implementing the *Arthaśāstra's* advice when he proposed an alliance to the Chinese whereby he would assist the Chinese in repelling the Japanese attack on Korea by invading the shores of his own enemy, the piratical Japanese king, in order to relieve Japanese pressure on Korea. Diplomatic flair probably came easily to rulers in multicentred Southeast Asia.

I have now suggested that Indian literary models, circulating over the single ocean, could provide possibilities for identifying a common cultural heritage in Southeast Asia as Henri Brugmans was able to do for Europe. We are still, of course, dealing with multiple, concurrent, and competitive élite groups rather than with a single, coherent, and cohesive élite. Nevertheless, we seem to be closer to an intra-regional communality of outlook, engendered by an intellectual predictability of behaviour among leaders of the various *maṇḍalas*. These influences, products of historical experience, could contribute to the shape of a genuinely "Southeast Asian" history.

A sense of universal standards of excellence, a present-mindedness of outlook, and participation in a common fund of Indian-derived literature are "Southeast Asian" cultural features which occurred to me after trying to respond to Henri Brugmans' discussion of the "European heritage". This line of thought may be bringing me quite

28. Jean Boisselier, *La Statuaire du Champa*, pp. 241–43.
29. B.R. Chatterji, *History of Indonesia*, p. 183, v. 29.

century had special reasons for wanting to preserve the country's cultural identity; for example, in 1374 an edict was issued to warn people, presumably living in the disturbed border regions, not to "copy the speech of the Chams and Lao". But what is significant in the account of Nhật Duật is that the Cham prisoners were still recognized as culturally different after more than two centuries in exile. The exiles' retention of their customs and language is a reminder of two influences which, more than anything else, validate the proposition that Southeast Asia is a region of extreme cultural diversity: society and language.

I shall refer only very briefly to the variety of social structures in the region. When I sketched the cultural matrix, I indicated a few traits which I supposed would be widespread, but I am well aware of notable exceptions. For example, the Minangkabau and Chams practise matrilineal descent, while the Bataks, Balinese, and Muong practise patrilineal descent. Even where cognatic kinship exists, the societies are by no means similar in all respects: the nuclear family is not necessarily the basic group; marriage, death, and burial rites are not uniform. The attribution of "prowess" is explained by all kinds of personal and external forces. The least we can do is to take it for granted that society was variously organized in earlier Southeast Asia. Groups and individuals would not have behaved in identical ways. Manpower would not have been deployed on similar lines everywhere. There could also have been different rates of population growth.

But the clinching evidence of cultural diversity is provided by the many different languages used in the region, even though they can be grouped into several families. When we think of them, we have to bear in mind what de Saussure says of "language": "it is both a social product of the faculty of speech and a collection of necessary conventions that have been adopted by a social body to permit individuals to exercise the faculty".[47] A language expresses a social collectivity in the form of idiosyncratic relationships and differences between its linguistic units.[48]

Bayard, "Comment", *Early Southeast Asia*, pp. 278–80. A notable example of ethnic and linguistic fluidity is mentioned by E.R. Leach, *Political systems of Highland Burma*, p. 40, where he maintains that various hill peoples in Burma, such as the Kachin, gradually became Shan. For a study of the contrasting ability of the Thai and Javanese to assimilate Chinese, see G. William Skinner, "Change and persistence in Chinese culture overseas: a comparison of Thailand and Java", *Journal of the South Seas Society* 16, no. 1–2 (Singapore, 1960): 86–100.

47. Ferdinand de Saussure, *Course in General Linguistics*, p. 9.
48. Ibid., pp. 120–22.

Linguistic cultural identity becomes particularly visible when we note what happened to Sanskrit loan words. De Saussure is again helpful: "a loan word no longer counts as such whenever it is studied within a [linguistic] system; it exists only through its relation with, and opposition to, words associated with it ...".[49] For example, the Javanese naturalized the Sanskrit word *santosa*, which means "contemplation" and "satisfaction", to signify what was important to them: the ideal state of mind of "the completely unconcerned" man in control of all passions.[50] The Javanese language, expressing a Javanese social collectivity, has appropriated the word *santosa* and given it a non-Indian meaning. The loan word is now an Old-Javanese word, for the Sanskrit word in question does not seem to have the same linguistic status in any other Indonesian language. J. Gonda observes that Sanskrit abstract words with religious and ethical significance were often expressed in "a specifically Javanese manner",[51] an observation which, in itself, tells us something about this culture and can help us to distinguish it from other cultures within the Austronesian family of languages.

Observing how Sanskrit loan words fitted into the local languages is one way of recognizing the presence of what Quaritch Wales calls "local genius". Loan words cannot be assumed to have similar shifts in meaning in every Southeast Asian language. In the Khmer language the Sanskrit word *siddhi*, or "success", could also mean "the exclusive right to village revenues",[52] but Gonda's *Sanskrit in Indonesia* does not mention this usage. In Javanese, the Sanskrit word *śakti*, or "the creating power of divinities, etc.", came to signify "supernatural power", whereas in Toba Batak *sokti* expresses the idea of "whose pronouncements or predictions are borne out by the facts or verified (of a magician)".[53] In Bali, *śakti* is identified with "ancestral power".[54]

So much for a few glimpses of the bewildering differences to be studied in this region of cultural diversity. Only one conclusion seems reasonable. Much more historical and anthropological research is

49. Ibid., p. 22. The Chinese word for "pavilion" or "village" (*t'ing*), pronounced as *đình* in Vietnam, became the word used for the Vietnamese village communal house and centre for worshipping local heroes and heroines. The god of an ancient volcanic mountain cult in Java was identified as Brahmā Svayambhū; see de Casparis, "Pour une histoire sociale de l'ancienne Java principalement au Xème s", p. 143.
50. J. Gonda, *Sanskrit in Indonesia*, p. 203.
51. Ibid., 202.
52. For example, see George Coedès, *IC* 2, p. 66, v. 1–5.
53. J. Gonda, op. cit., p. 65.
54. James A. Boon, *The Anthropological Romance of Bali*, p. 133.

necessary before sufficient is known about the geographical spans of the subregional cultures, their nuances, the extent to which they overlapped and influenced each other, and the ways in which they might have altered during historical times. In the meantime, historians can be alert to signs of distinctive cultural traits in the areas of their competence and, when feasible, make cautious comparisons with what is known of other areas. The concept of "earlier Southeast Asia" is helpful because it invites us to keep abreast of all subregional studies for comparative purposes. But detailed historical research in particular subregions is what is needed most, and broad generalizations about a "Southeast Asian" culture must be avoided. As Donald K. Emmerson notes, cross-cultural generalizations reduce "the capacity to distinguish Southeast Asia from other world regions".[55] Generalizations are even more unfortunate when they blur subregional differences.

I have attempted in this chapter to define the subject known as "earlier Southeast Asian history". Criticism may arise especially from my doubt whether, in our present state of knowledge, the subject is much more than a will o' the wisp. How can regional history be organized around the theme of cultural diversity when one cannot present the theme in more than general terms or explain its historical implications for the region as a whole? The same kind of difficulties arise even when one is attempting the less ambitious project of writing "national" histories in the region. Taufik Abdullah insists that what is studied in local history must depend on what is significant in the development of the area in question. In the Indonesian historical context, the difference between local and national history is one of orientation. A "national" history does not represent a less detailed and more generalized treatment of "local" history:

> If national history seeks after a problematic which has as its aim the integration of the different localities, local history is unnecessary. A local problem is local, and all related matters revolve around it. Therefore the principal question [in local history] is simpler: can these matters, process, and structural tendencies clarify the development of a society in this area or this locality?[56]

I agree. Whether in Indonesia or elsewhere the locality or subregion should remain the focus for studying history in earlier Southeast Asia

55. Donald K. Emmerson, "Issues in Southeast Asian History: Room for Interpretation — a Review Article", *JAS* 40, no. 1 (1980): 51.
56. Taufik Abdullah, *Sejarah Lokal di Indonesia*, p. 14.

even though the region lay astride the communications of "the single ocean" and Indian literature reached its multiple landfalls.

The question now, as I see it, is not how to define earlier Southeast Asian history but to consider what the historian can do to study its salient feature, which is cultural diversity. Each historian will go his own way. My point of departure will be what happened to Indian materials when they arrived in this congeries of subregions unaccompanied by Indian-style brahmans,[57] and my approach is foreshadowed by my comments on what happened to Sanskrit loan words, represented in many of the local languages.

I believe, unless there is convincing evidence to the contrary, that Indian materials tended to be fractured and restated and therefore drained of their original significance by a process which I shall refer to as "localization". The materials, be they words, sounds of words, books, or artifacts, had to be localized in different ways before they could fit into various local complexes of religious, social, and political systems and belong to new cultural "wholes". Only when this had happened would the fragments make sense in their new ambiences, the same ambiences which allowed the rulers and their subjects to believe that their centres were unique.[58]

---

57. India was also multicentred, but the hereditary and mobile class of brahmans taught in the *maṭhas*, the equivalent of broadcasting stations, and were able to communicate new philosophical and devotional messages, originally articulated in southern India, and bring them to the most distant parts of the subcontinent. The brahmans, at least in theory, were a priestly society. Their *dharma* knew no boundaries on the map; *dharma* was wherever brahman society was believed to be represented. In Southeast Asia space was organized under cover of personal relationships between rulers and subjects and the priests were also subjects. The Southeast Asian "brahmans" never became the independent custodians and teachers of sacred texts. A further difference between India and Southeast Asia was that, on account of the Bay of Bengal, the relationship between the Sanskritic centres in India and their adjacent tribal areas does not automatically furnish formulae for studying the relationship between India and Southeast Asia. For a discussion of the relationship between "high" and "low" cultures in India, see I.W. Mabbett, "The 'Indianization' of Southeast Asia: Reflections on the Historical Sources", *JSEAS* 8, no. 2 (1977): 158–61.

58. I do not suppose that local cultural systems remained unchanged when they had localized foreign materials. My point of departure is what happened when foreign materials were originally localized. Even then, the host culture could not have been unaffected. For example, in the second section of the essay I suggested that in protohistoric times the chiefs' construction of Hindu devotionalism, based on local notions of "soul stuff" and "prowess", led to heightened self-perceptions among the chieftain class and prepared the ground for overlords' claims to universal sovereignty, based on Śiva's divine authority. In the lowlands, over the centuries local cultural features persisted in in-

We can now take leave of Henri Brugmans, who stimulated me in searching for a shape to regional history. Brugmans writes of the perpetual local "variations" on a few common "European" themes, but the situation in Southeast Asia is reversed: "variations" becomes an inappropriate expression, while independent "localizations", under the influence of different subregional cultures, become the common theme. For Brugmans, the common European themes are more easily seen from a distance than close at hand. In Southeast Asia, what is seen from a distance is similar modes of *maṇḍala* behaviour, with their origins in prehistory. What is seen close at hand is by no means clear but more significant: the product of history in the form of multifarious constructions of foreign materials that varied according to the part of the region we are studying and, because of the influence of the local cultures, would not have encouraged a region-wide awareness of a common "Indian" heritage.

In the following chapter I shall illustrate what I mean by "localization", but I want to give one example now. I have mentioned earlier that the *maṇḍalas*, which seem to offer a convenient framework for subregional histories, might, in some instances, have had a cultural outreach more lasting than their political influence. However, even this possibility for cultural outreach needs to be qualified. Not only did Indian materials have to be localized everywhere but those which had been originally localized in one part of the region would have to

---

creasingly complex religious and social systems, and each society localized foreign materials and conceptions at particular points in time and at particular stages in its own development. Changes in local cultural features are bound to have occurred. Phya Anuman Rajadhon suggests that an ancient Thai word for "soul" (*khwan*) shed this meaning in favour of the Pali-derived term *vinyan*, or "consciousness"; see "The Khwan and its Ceremonies", *Journal of the Siam Society* 50, no. 2 (1962): 120–22. In chapter 4, note 2, I mention Kirsch's suggestion of how local and foreign elements were "universalized" and "parochialized" respectively. Some of the examples of localization mentioned in Chapter 4 presuppose long periods of time when both local and foreign elements were changing. The processes behind the endless elaboration of new local-foreign cultural "wholes" is a subject for historians and anthropologists alike. However, I hold the view that local beliefs, operating under cultural constraint, were always responsible for the initial form the new "wholes" took.

"Adaptation", "synthesis", and especially "syncretism" are sometimes used to describe the process I refer to as "localization". These terms seem to shirk the crucial question of where and how foreign elements began to fit into a local culture. "Adaptation" and "synthesis" give an impression of the outcome of the process, while "syncretism" does likewise and also begs the question by conveying a dictionary sense of reconciliation of originally contradictory differences. The three terms smother the initiative of the local elements responsible for the process and the end product.

be relocalized before they could belong elsewhere in the same subregion. The process of re-localization is another opportunity for studying cultural diversity.

Zoetmulder describes the deep respect Balinese scholars in modern times have for Old-Javanese literature.[59] Yet, Old-Javanese "Hindu-Buddhist" traditions had to fit into a different cultural tradition even in this neighbouring island. James Boon suggests that the Javanese courtly way of life was top heavy on the small island of Bali and that its influence spilled downwards to the "middling families". The Javanese emphasis on hierarchy had to make allowances for Balinese values, and the effect is what Boon calls a "romance" in the sense that "romance is a popularization that embraces vernacular concerns, a compromise between courtly standards and the surrounding subliterate world".[60] The Balinese world where Old-Javanese materials were relocalized was influenced by its own processes of social change. Moreover, the Balinese sense of romantic adventure and the shifts and tensions in their religious and political hierarchy played their part in transforming Javanese influences.[61] One consequence can be seen in the Balinese versions of the Javanese Panji tales which "articulate a distinctly Balinese marriage system and a perhaps Oceanic value on individual love".[62] A similar study could be made of relocalized Angkorian materials in Ayudhyā, with its focus less on the extent of Angkorian influence than on the information the relocalizing process supplies about Thai culture.

I am not offering "localization" as a historian's gimmick or even as an original idea[63] but because the term seems to have a bearing on the subject of this essay, from which the attempt to define regional history has distracted me: culture, history, and region in Southeast Asian perspectives. I believe that the term is a helpful one in studying local cultural differences in historical perspective. I am not sug-

---

59. P.J. Zoetmulder, op. cit., pp. 36–50.
60. James A. Boon, *The Anthropological Romance of Bali*, pp. 3–4.
61. Ibid., p. 5.
62. Ibid., p. 7.
63. W.F. Stutterheim is the best known scholar with this perspective. His studies are outlined by J.G. de Casparis in "Historical writing on Indonesia (early period)", *Historians of South East Asia*, pp. 138–40. Benda was thinking on the same lines when he enquired whether one means of identifying a common Southeast Asian culture would be to identify "modifications in transplanted Indian and Chinese patterns respectively" which "could be traced to common, or at least similar, indigenous factors"; see Harry Benda, "The Structure of Southeast Asian History", *Journal of Southeast Asia History* 3, no. 1 (1962): 111. I believe that Benda's approach would make us more sensitive to differences among the local cultures themselves.

gesting, of course, that what happened to foreign materials is the only central theme for historical enquiry. On the other hand, because foreign materials found their way to many subregions, the historian has the opportunity of asking himself questions about the local host societies, thrown into relief by the process of localization, and about differences between them. In Mary Wright's words,[64] here is one means of opening up "ranges of experience" in Southeast Asia, bringing them into sharper focus, and investigating different cultural environments in which every significant happening and, indeed, every sequence of happenings was generated.

The term "localization" has the merit of calling our attention to something else outside the foreign materials. One way of conceptualizing "something else" is as a local statement, of cultural interest but not necessarily in written form, into which foreign elements have retreated. I shall give a few examples of particular local statements bearing on lines of enquiry discussed earlier. In some local statements, however, the foreign materials have retreated so completely that they seem to have disappeared, and the processes by which they do so provide a special opportunity for studying the cultural mosaic we call Southeast Asia.

64. Mary C. Wright, "Chinese History and the Historical Vocation", *JAS* 23, no. 4 (1964): 515.

CHAPTER FOUR

Local Cultural Statements

When I discussed the self-perceptions of the chieftain class in the protohistoric period, I suggested that the "Hindu" evidence in the inscriptions revealed religious *rapport* between leaders and led which could be explained by a pre-"Hindu" acknowledgement of different levels of prowess within the chieftain class. In Cambodia, where protohistoric evidence is relatively ample, an overlord's cult was the cult of the chief who was seen as having achieved the closest relationship with the god. This was why subordinate chiefs, with their own devotional cults, sometimes offered Śiva gifts that they had received from their overlord as tokens of their own devotion. Their "Hindu" devotion seems to have been heightened by their association with the overlord. The "Hindu" cults in honour of Śiva are therefore calling attention to a network of relationships in Khmer society.

The same evidence points to another local feature. Nidhi Aeusrivongse observes that a Cambodian inscription of AD 611 mentions a god whose name ends with *-īśvara*; the inscription is damaged, but the god is almost certainly Śiva.[1] The inscription records the merging of arrangements for maintaining the god's cult with those in honour of a sacred tree. Nidhi Aeusrivongse believes that this is an example of how a local spirit could find a place in the Hindu pantheon.[2] We do

1. Nidhi Aeusrivongse, "*Devarāja* Cult and Khmer Kingship at Angkor", *Explorations in Early Southeast Asia: the Origins of Southeast Asian Statecraft*, p. 115; and George Coedès, *Les Inscriptions du Cambodge* (hereafter cited as *IC*), vol. 2, pp. 21–23. On *-īśvara* see K. Bhattacharya, *Les religions brahmaniques das l'ancien Cambodge*, p. 125. See A. Barth and A. Bergaigne, *Inscriptions sancrites du Cambodge et Champa*, p. 388, for the possibility of a donation to an indigenous cult under the name of Sri Brahmarakśas.
2. Nidhi Aeusrivongse, op. cit. Kirsch discusses this kind of situation in a Thai context, and suggests that locality spirits were long ago identified, by a process

not know whether an overlord existed in 611, but later in the same century a ruler, who may have been the overlord Jayavarman I, ordered slaves to be conducted to a prominent chief and allocated among the ruler's sanctuaries in a certain area. The gods in question are described as sharing the "domain" of the tree spirit mentioned in the inscription of 611.[3] The tree spirit now has a direct relationship with an overlord as well as with "Hindu" gods. In this way, a local spirit could find its place not only in the "Hindu" pantheon but also in the network of social and political relationships around which seventh-century Khmer society was organized during periods of overlordship.

Here, then, is a possibility for studying a cultural statement into which foreign materials have retreated and begin to call attention to features of Khmer society. Quaritch Wales examines monumental art as an expression of "local genius" but doubts whether "social structure" can be similarly studied. The reason is that he agrees with Van Leur that "what expressions of Indian civilization there were in early Indonesia were without exception sacral".[4] But can any single aspect of a society be isolated as "sacral"? The evidence of seventh-century Cambodia suggests that a sharp distinction did not exist between "religious" and "secular" behaviour. No single Khmer had the monopoly of "Hindu" materials; the chieftain class as a whole was involved, and religious and political relationships between leaders and led overlapped. The foreign materials are bringing situations within this class to the foreground, and the class becomes a subject for further study.

Foreign materials were also dispersed in Malay society in south-eastern Sumatra during the later seventh century. According to the Sabokingking inscription at Palembang, the Sriwijayan ruler feared a regrouping of personal ties and alliances, and one of his concerns was that his enemies — no doubt other Malay chiefs — had magical

he calls "parochialisation", with the cosmological deities of Hinduism. The result was that "the deity is made less abstract and more on par with the indigenous system of beliefs. But such identifications simultaneously involve a process of universalisation. The familiar spirit, now identified with a more abstract and universal cosmological scheme, is upgraded to an entity more distant than previously"; see Thomas A. Kirsch, "Complexity in the Thai Religious System: An Interpretation", *Journal of Asian Studies* 36, no. 2 (1977): 263.

3. Nidhi Aeusrivongse, op. cit., p. 115; and George Coedès, *IC*, vol. 2, p. 117. Coedès notes that the name given to the slaves corresponds to a modern word for an "aboriginal population"; ibid., note 4.

4. Quaritch Wales, *The Making of Greater India*, p. 227. He goes on to say that "everywhere [in Southeast Asia] up to the end of the eighth century there was little scope for the local peoples to express themselves in their own way in the official art and religion"; ibid., p. 230.

"tantric" means at their disposal which they could employ for subversive purposes.[5] But tantric materials may tell us about more than stresses and strains in Sriwijayan society. The ruler, too, possessed tantric means to strengthen his influence. He promised a *tantrāmala* to those who did not break their oath of allegiance. The word used for "oath" is a Malay one (*sumpah*), and the oath's sanctions permeate the inscription's contents. Perhaps the ruler was offering something as familiar to Malays as the royal oath he was administering. J.G. de Casparis, who edited the inscription, suggests that *tantrāmala* should be rendered literally as "immaculate as a consequence of Tantra" and that it could be a specific object such as a metal plate or clay tablet on which sacred words were written.[6] If sacred words were inscribed in this way, and even if the words were incomprehensible to most recipients, the localized foreign materials could be enhancing the value Malays were accustomed to attribute to royal gifts, so often mentioned in later Malay literature.

Outlines of cultural statements about two societies in action in seventh-century Cambodia and Sumatra are available but they could not be discerned without the assistance of Śaivite and tantric fragments. Another example of a localizing process is found in an almost anonymous society but one in which something happened under cultural constraint.

Tom Harrisson and Stanley O'Connor excavated a small tantric shrine in Santubong in western Sarawak.[7] Santubong is one of several landfalls in this part of the Borneo coast, and iron-ore was being worked nearby as early as at least the seventh or eighth century. The shrine possesses a ritual deposit chamber and may be an instance of the Javanese *maṇḍala's* cultural outreach. The Brunei ruler was a Majapahit vassal in the middle of the fourteenth century, and the shrine is believed to have been constructed in the thirteenth or fourteenth century. The shrine's interest lies, however, in the circumstance that it was found in an area where the cultural horizon is dominated by burial practices and the carving of rocks, which are outside Indian tradition. The shrine was clearly connected with tantric ritual prescriptions, yet it was covered by a random collection of shale which is reminiscent of the inhabitants' reverence for heaped pebbles. The shale cover had to be above the shrine in order to give what most of the population probably regarded as the stamp of

5. J.G. de Casparis, *Prasasti Indonesia, II*, pp. 15–46.
6. Ibid., p. 31, notes 55 and 56.
7. Tom Harrisson and Stanley J. O'Connor, *Gold and Megalithic Activity in Prehistoric and Recent West Borneo.*

sanctity on whatever religious associations the shrine had for those influenced by tantric notions. The shale and deposit chamber are fitting into a cultural statement in the same way that the *tantrāmala* and the royal gift may be fitting in seventh-century Sumatra.

Boon, an anthropologist, provides the next example of a local statement; it concerns what eventually happened in Bali to the two major Hindu gods, Śiva and Viṣṇu.[8] C. Hooykaas has emphasized a number of features of Balinese "Hinduism" which cannot be accounted for by Indian influences. For example, the Balinese believe that one is reborn within one's group of blood-relatives, that the gods live above the mountains and lakes and are not present day and night in the temples, and that cremation should be practised only if one's social position justifies it. Above all, the Balinese attach a "preponderant importance" to the Holy Waters".[9] Not surprisingly then, Śiva and Viṣṇu, though they have not entirely shed attributes derived from their Indian origins, fit into a new environment in Bali. They now enjoy a Balinese complementary relationship.

Śiva continues to represent "sacralised and stable authority" or "kingly authority and religious purity". Viṣṇu's localization is more interesting. Boon believes that in Bali Viṣṇu represents the "rising prince", evidently an echo of the Indian perception of Viṣṇu as the god who periodically reincarnates himself to protect the world from crumbling. But the Balinese conception of Viṣṇu's occasions for reappearing is a local one. The god represents "infusions of new religious and status energies from the periphery". The Balinese cultural background is one in which new men appear from time to time from the fringes of extensive and ascendant ancestor-groups, build up networks of alliances by demonstrating their capacity for leadership, and eventually become Ancestors in a particular generation by virtue of their achievements during their lifetime on behalf of their kindred. Localization in Bali means that Viṣṇu's periodic reappearances fit into a Balinese statement constrained by local mechanisms for social mobilization. Viṣṇu has thus retreated into Balinese society.[10]

---

8. James A. Boon, *The Anthropological Romance of Bali*, pp. 197–205.
9. C. Hooykaas, *Religion in Bali*, p. 25.
10. Donn Hart's study of ritual kinship in the Philippines illustrates how the Catholic institution of godparenthood was rapidly localized. Hart notes that "a sympathetic convergence occurred between indigenous cultural traits and the godparenthood complex"; see Donn V. Hart, *Compadrinazgo, Ritual Kinship in the Philippines*, p. 50. He compares the situation with that in Latin America, where numerous differences can be found.

Localized foreign materials do not have to be Indian to tell us something about a society. R.C. Ileto's study of Tagalog society in the nineteenth and early twentieth centuries reveals that the associations of the Christian Holy Week were construed in terms of the Filipino concept of *loób*, the inner self and a force with power to attract followers.[11] Here, as in Bali, we have a cultural statement about the mechanism of mobilization and, in this instance, for a grave purpose. The Tagalog peasants believed that those whose *loób* was "pure, serene, and controlled, have special powers granted to them by Christ", and the result was that, towards the end of the Spanish regime, their leaders, who were perceived in this way, enacted the roles of Christ and His disciples and organized armed rebellion in defiance of the colonial authorities. Leaders were sometimes expected to appear as Tagalog "kings", for Christ was hailed as "King" during the *pasyon* week. "Surely," remarks Ileto, "the friars did not intend the *pasyon* themes of self-purification and renewal to amplify notions of concentrating the 'creative' energy of the universe in one's *loób*. But, in the end, the colonised had their way."[12]

The next example has a magnificence of foreign materials but the materials point to something else. Eleanor Moron has undertaken an extraordinarily detailed analysis of the celestial arithmetic which provides the spatial and temporal framework of Angkor Wat, built during the reign of Sūryavarman II of Cambodia in the first half of the twelfth century.[13] Her exact and convincing evidence, based on the measurements within the temple complex, reveals that "Angkor Wat expands westward and eastward through the *kṛta yuga* time period. The visitor crosses into the *kṛta yuga* when entering the temple on the west and crosses out of it when leaving in the east. The visitor also walks into the *kṛta yuga* when entering the gallery of bas-relief".[14] And so, when one enters the complex, one is turning one's back on the present and deteriorating age, the *kali yuga*, and returning to the first or golden age, represented by the king's reign. The bas-relief around the galleries consistently depicts this happy dispensation from the time when Sūryavarman, still very young, seized the throne from two kings, one of whom was his aged uncle, quelled a civil war, and went on to regenerate a *maṇḍala* that eventually

11. Reynaldo C. Ileto, *Pasyon and Revolution. Popular Movements in the Philippines, 1840–1911*.
12. Ibid., p. 33.
13. Eleanor Moron, "Configurations of time and space at Angkor Wat", *Studies in Indo-Asian Art and Culture* 5 (1977): 217–67.
14. Ibid., p. 220.

extended from Nghệ-an in Vietnam[15] to the Chao Phraya basin. On the southern half of the western face of the gallery we see the frightful battle scene of Kurukṣetra, borrowed from the *Mahābhārata*. On the southern face we see the king's dead enemies and supporters; they are descending into the underworld to be judged. The eastern face shows the king as Yama, the judge of the dead, which is Viṣṇu's role in a passage in the *Mahābhārata*.[16] Also on the eastern face, we see Viṣṇu churning creative ambrosia to sustain the golden age after the dust of battle has settled. The northern face shows a constellation of planets, and Moron was able to calculate the date when the sanctuary image was consecrated; the ceremony occurred during the end of July 1131.[17]

Hindu cosmogony and the Hindu epic have supplied the great monument with its spatial and temporal frame, and Viṣṇu, the reincarnating god, has provided what Moron calls a "divine metaphor, meant to exalt but not deify the king".[18] In Southeast Asia as well as in India, the Viṣṇu metaphor was commonly used for eulogising the king.[19] The Javanese king Erlangga and "the rising prince" in the Balinese ancestor groups were rendered in this way. Similarly, the view was held in Southeast Asia as well as in India that the king was the maker of his "age" (*yuga*). The Cham ruler who supported his accession to the throne by writing a Sanskrit treatise resembling a *smṛti* also claimed that Champa was in the *kṛta yuga*, or golden age.[20]

The Indian conventions of Viṣṇu and the golden age, so exuberantly deployed in Angkor Wat, do not in themselves, however, comprise the monument's cultural statement. The conventions draw attention to something else that is Khmer. Some Khmer elements are unambiguous. The monument's short inscriptions refer to "Lvo" and

15. See *Dại Việt sũ-ký toàn thu- (TT)* under the dates of 1128, 1132, and 1127. Nghệ-an was raided twice in 1128, and the Khmer king demanded that Vietnamese envoys should be sent to Cambodia. The demand was rejected. The raid in 1132 was by Khmers and Chams.

16. F.D.K. Bosch, "Notes archéologiques. IV. Le temple d'Ankor Vat", *Bulletin de l'École Française d'Extrême-Orient (BEFEO)* 32 (1932): 16.

17. Moron, op. cit., p. 233. "The astronomers apparently used Angkor Wat itself as a kind of observatory"; ibid., p. 245.

18. Ibid., p. 221, note 7.

19. For example, see A. Barth and A. Bergaigne, op. cit., p. 68, v. 2; George Coedès, *IC*, vol. 1, p. 15, v. 4; J. Gonda. *Aspects of early Visnuism*, pp. 164–65.

20. L. Finot, "Notes d'épigraphie XI: Les inscriptions de Mi-so-n", *BEFEO* 4 (1904): 958, v. 16, and p. 961, v. 16. For Cambodian references to the golden age, see, for example, George Coedès, *IC*, vol. 4, p. 23, v. 8; and p. 227, v. 77. On the golden age in Indian literature, see U.N. Ghoshal, *A History of Indian Political Ideas*, pp. 164, 199.

"Syām", Khmer captives or vassals from the Chao Phraya basin. The dates Moron has been able to decipher are Khmer ones. The identification of Sūryavarman with Yama, the judge of the dead, is in the Khmer and also the Southeast Asian cultural traditional, for obedience and disobedience to the king had consequences in the afterlife. As one Cambodian inscription puts it, "kingship should be honoured by those who enjoy good works".[21] Merit-earning conduct on the ruler's behalf promoted the subject's prospects of spiritual rewards, and this was why seventh-century Khmer chiefs would transfer the king's gifts to Śiva. In 1011, the corps of inspectors (*tamrvāc*) of Sūryavarman I took an oath which ended thus: "May we obtain the recompense of people devoted to our masters in this and the other world".[22]

What, then, is the Khmer statement embodied in Angkor Wat? I believe the key is signified in the southern panel on the western wall, where the series of bas-relief begins. The panel shows the Kurukṣetra battle. This battle in traditional Indian cosmogony introduced the last age of the world, and Bosch notes that in Java, and apparently in Cambodia too, the battle was considered to be an inauspicious event and was avoided as a topic for bas-relief.[23] In Angkor Wat, however, the battle has been localized to introduce the golden age and, in the eyes of those responsible for the monument, the golden age was still in being. The king was not yet dead. Angkor Wat is therefore a spectacular formulation of the privilege of living in Sūryavarman's generation, when internal peace was restored and Khmer military forces, with plentiful chances for personal achievement, marched to the extremities of mainland Southeast Asia. The monument, with its wealth of foreign materials, points to this privilege.

Angkor Wat resembles a statement one can envisage in a society that practised cognatic kinship, where the relative unimportance of lineage and the attribution of special spiritual qualities to leaders inculcated an alertness in reading contemporary signs and, in this case, embodying them in stone. The signifiers visible at Angkor Wat are drawn from Indian literature, but they signify a Khmer formulation associated with the Khmers' expectations of being

---

21. George Coedès, "La stele de Prasat Komnap", *BEFEO* 32, no. 1 (1932): 94, v. 27.
22. George Coedès, *IC*, vol. 3, p. 210.
23. F.D.K. Bosch, op. cit., pp. 13–14. The Pandawas' kingdom of Amarta in Javanese *wayang kulit* provides another example of a localized rendering of Indian epic materials. The short period of Pandawa rule over the kingdom gets little attention in the Indian epic, but not so in Java; see James R. Brandon, ed., *On Thrones of Gold. Three Javanese Shadow Plays*, pp. 11–14.

Sūryavarman's contemporaries. Angkor Wat is an example of a local statement into which Indian conventions of Viṣṇu and the golden age have retreated so completely that they have become, in a literal sense, decorative. The expression "cultural statement" can even be suitably replaced by the expression "text", or something that has to be read. The literary repertoire is certainly Indian, but the "literary" effect of the Khmers' combination of Indian decorative elements, beginning with Kurukṣetra, has to be recovered before the monument's statement can be read as a Khmer one.

Vietnam offers more straightforward instances of foreign materials retreating into local statements. Chinese literary materials were as familiar to educated Vietnamese as Indian ones were to the architects of Angkor Wat, and passages from Chinese literature, or even fragments, are frequently found in Vietnamese writings. So localized had Chinese literature become in Vietnam that it even supplied diplomatic weaponry against the Chinese themselves. The Vietnamese court had plenty of occasions for reminding the Northern court of the Chinese dogma that an ideal ruler should show a benign attitude towards distant peoples. Vietnamese memorials to China often alluded to the dogma as an argument for dissuading the emperors from infringing Vietnamese sovereignty.

A more interesting example of the way foreign materials could retreat into local statements as completely as they did at Angkor Wat is seen in 1127, when the dying ruler, Lý Nhân-tôn, chose to formalize his choice of an heir by reproducing, with only a few and necessary deviations, the death-bed edict issued by the Han emperor, Wên-ti (180-157 BC). The literary decoration of Nhân-tôn's edict is recognizably Chinese, but the statement itself, uttered in urgent circumstances, is his own. Childless, he intended to appoint as his heir a young nephew, whom he had earlier adopted as his son, even though the recently established dynastic system of government had hitherto depended on the succession of vigorous adult sons. The impending crisis facing the dynastic institution required a special death-bed edict, and this was why the ruler enclosed his edict within a famous piece of Chinese literature so that it would call special attention to his message. Every member of his court would have been able to read the edict as Nhân-tôn intended, which was that the nephew was as qualified to succeed him as emperor Wên-ti had wanted his heir to be, as it is recorded in another famous piece of Chinese literature. Nhân-tôn was representing himself as being as conscientious as Wên-ti, in spite of the fact that his situation was different from Wên-ti's in one respect; Wên-ti had sought a worthy heir early in his reign, whereas the Lý rulers always postponed the formal announcement of their intention until they were dying.

Nevertheless, Nhân-tôn knew that his courtiers shared the Vietnamese literary convention that famous fragments of Chinese literature were endowed with timeless wisdom. Nhân-tôn was using literary authority to secure his young heir's succession to the throne, and his edict can be seen as a local cultural statement that calls attention to the novelty and perhaps fragility of the Vietnamese dynastic institution.[24]

A similar literary convention can be found in 1258, when the Buddhist ruler Trần Thái-tôn wanted to protect the imperial succession at a time of danger after the first Mongol invasion. He incorporated the name of the Chinese sage and ruler Yao in his title to communicate his prescience in nominating an heir when he himself was still in the prime of life and his heir had reached the age of eighteen.[25] Yao was admired by Mencius for showing the same prescience, and the allusion to Mencius provides Thái-tôn with an eloquent equivalence and the same kind of authority that Nhân-tôn had invoked by alluding to Wên-ti's edict. Again, in 1272 a Vietnamese official assembled several Chinese philosophical and historical fragments, some of which he took out of their original context, in order to demonstrate the antiquity of the Vietnamese imperial institution which Thái-tôn and his heir were defending against Kubilai Khan. The Chinese fragments are tailored to fit into Vietnamese history and show that Vietnam's tributary relationship with China was a fiction.[26]

In these Vietnamese examples, as in the case of Angkor Wat's Indian fragments, Chinese materials provide a quality of "literariness" that helps to communicate local statements. The fragments do no more than contribute to the formulation of the meaning of the Vietnamese and Khmer "texts". The precise "literary" contribution of the fragments is a matter of interpretation. I have chosen to refer to their "decorative" effect in Angkor Wat. Chinese fragments in Vietnam, associated with the prestige of antiquity, were certainly rhetorical. In Java, Sanskrit fragments contributed to local texts in other ways. In Old-Javanese *parwa* literature the quotations often occur "in the very middle of a sentence without being integrated into it".[27] Sanskrit quotations may have provided "an atmosphere of

24. O.W. Wolters, "Historians and Emperors in Vietnam and China", *Perceptions of the Past in Southeast Asia*, p. 81.
25. Ibid., pp. 79–80.
26. Ibid., p. 86.
27. P.J. Zoetmulder, *Kalangwan*, p. 89.

solemnity" because they were often didactic maxims,[28] or lent an aura of "authoritativeness".[29]

Foreign fragments, therefore, are fitting one way or another into new contexts. My inventory of examples is miscellaneous, but the vocabulary I, and those whom I quoted, have used to describe the localizing processes has not been unsystematic. The vocabulary is similar to that used for describing "literary" effects. The "literariness" of the localizing process is clearest in respect of Angkor Wat. Moron identifies Viṣṇu as a "metaphor" for exalting Sūryavarman. Hindu cosmogony and epic literature, supplying the monument with its spatial and temporal frame, provide "equivalences" of the golden age and also add "decorative" effects which enable the Khmers to "formulate" their privileged sensation of living in Sūryavarman's generation. The "signifiers" visible at Angkor Wat mean something else to the Khmers and enable them to communicate their own message. These ways of describing the monument belong to a mode of analysis which would equally well be used in analysing a written text. The Vietnamese deploy Chinese fragments for "rhetorical" purposes, and this is another term for describing a literary effect.

Even in the other instances of localization, the effect of the foreign fragments can be rendered in terms appropriate in literary criticism. The Sriwijayan ruler's *tantrāmala* may have enhanced the value Malays attributed to a royal gift, while Ileto uses the term "amplify" when he brings the *pasyon* themes into relation with the Tagalog peasants' notions of *loób*. In both cases the term "intensify", used for language effects, would be equally satisfactory. The *tantrāmala* can also be regarded as the "equivalence" of a royal gift. I suggested that the Santubong shale cover put a local stamp of sanctity on whatever religious associations the tantric shrine had. I could have said "intensified". Those who wrote the Old-Javanese *parwa* may have used Sanskrit fragments for the sake of their magical sounds; sound produces literary effect. In Bali, the difference between Śiva and Viṣṇu corresponds with the gods' relationship in India, but the one takes the form of an arrived leader (Śiva) while the other is beginning to arrive from the periphery (Viṣṇu). In Saussurian linguistics, to which I shall refer below, importance is attached to relationships and differences, and the same importance is reflected in literary studies.

The foreign elements in these examples tend to shrink to the status of quasi-"literary" devices, and in each case their effectiveness has to be identified before a local statement about something else can be

28. Ibid., p. 91.
29. Ibid., p. 92.

discovered. The fragments have submitted to the influence of local cultural statements and need to be read alongside other elements in the statements just as one does when one reads words on a page. Indeed, I have referred to Angkor Wat as a "text". The Vietnamese examples are unquestionably texts; even Trần Thái-tôn's title is a text. Therefore, one way of thinking about the cultural mosaic we call "Southeast Asia" may be as a mosaic of local "literary cultures" in the sense that foreign and local features are fitting into various text-like wholes.

I have been broaching a process for restoring the effects of foreign fragments when they retreat into local cultural ambiences, but my examples do not shed light on instances of the cultural diversity sustaining the multicentred landscape of earlier Southeast Asia. If literary terminology is to be helpful in studying how foreign elements functioned in different local cultures, the proper place for this approach must surely be the Southeast Asian literatures themselves, by which I mean epigraphic records as well as any other surviving specimens of writing.

I shall pause with this possibility. I had responded to a seminar invitation because it gave me an unexpected opportunity for doing something I had not attempted before, which was to reflect on the shape of history in the region. I began by suggesting that, when historical records first appeared in the early centuries of the Christian era, there were numerous scattered centres of population. The inhabitants spoke various languages but were likely in many areas to have independently exhibited a few similar cultural features associated with cognatic kinship systems. The salient feature was an ability to identify and rally behind spiritually endowed leaders in specific generations, which meant that local societies could be mobilized for intra-regional adventures. This situation projected itself into the historical period, when records commemorated the exploits of the well-known *maṇḍalas*, or "circles of kings". The reality, however, was that those who lived in a *maṇḍala* centre were convinced that their centre was "unique". Intra-regional relations were not conducted on the basis of equality among the centres.

I then enquired whether Brugman's rendering of Europe as a region of "perpetual variations on a relatively restricted number of themes" provided a helpful model for characterizing earlier Southeast Asian history. The continuous flow of foreign materials, especially Indian ones, over the single ocean's always open communications could have introduced regionally shared themes which, in historical times, offset the multicentred way of life inherited from prehistory. I suggested several influences making for a region-wide communality of outlook, at least among the élite: an awareness of universal values, emphasized in Indian literature; the example of Indian models for organizing knowledge; and a propensity for modernity that came from an outward looking disposition encouraged by easy maritime communications, and predisposing the élite to expect the arrival of new and updated ideas with the stamp of universal standards of excellent behaviour. In these ways the élite could gradually become impressed by what they seemed to share in common with the rest of the civilized world to which Indian literature addressed itself. In these ways something approaching a "Southeast Asian" predictability of outlook could have been engendered by the acknowledgement of a common fount of Indian conceptions.

This possibility was not very different from Coedès's presentation of "the Hinduised states of Southeast Asia", but I immediately rejected his presentation because it diverted us from the study of the region for its own sake. I preferred an approach which took as its point of departure the region's cultural diversity, concealed by *maṇḍala* history. The nature and extent of cultural diversity were elusive, but there was sufficient historical evidence to justify the expression, though the clinching evidence was provided by language diversity. I therefore concluded that the shape of the subject must accommodate this conspicuous characteristic and that the subject should be studied as the histories of numerous cultural subregions. The historian's responsibility was the study of this or that culture without allowing himself to be preoccupied by the problem of organizing a regional shape to the subject.

The question now was how the historian should approach the study of cultural diversity. One approach was to enquire what happened to Indian materials circulating in different subregions, and I suggested that they were "localized" in different ways to become part of the local cultures just as Sanskrit loan words were localized. I also suggested that the presence of foreign elements could interest historians because it was throwing into sharper relief the "something else" in the local cultures responsible for the localizing process. Foreign and local elements belonged to what I called "local cultural statements", though the pattern of localization could not be uniform throughout the region.

I gave a few examples of local statements, and this led me to compare them with literary statements. The function of foreign elements could be described in terms appropriate for identifying literary effects. The possibility therefore arose that the study of local literatures would itself contribute to a sharper definition of cultural particularities. An enquiry on these lines might be a step towards a comparative study of the literatures and a further elucidation of the cultural mosaic and shape of history in earlier Southeast Asia.

I have reached this conclusion after a roundabout discussion, and I could end here. I have not done so because I want to say something about what I mean by literary study or, more exactly, textual study. Perhaps the topic does not belong to an essay originally conceived on more general lines but, for two reasons, I have decided to extend its scope. Firstly, historians of Southeast Asia have always been hospitable to a variety of research tools. Textual study is another tool, and its orientations have, I believe, a close bearing on the study of cultural diversity. Language use is the foundation of any culture, and it deserves its place in a discussion of regional history where the focus has come to rest on cultural diversity. Secondly, textual study is concerned with literary processes. What is studied is how writers in particular cultures used language to produce meaning. The making of literature is one of the processes at work in earlier Southeast Asia, and all historical processes are the historian's concern.

CHAPTER FIVE

Local Literatures

The literatures of earlier Southeast Asia are not usually studied for textual purposes. Inscriptions, for example, are examined for documentary information referring to something outside themselves, such as an event which matches related information found in other inscriptions, monuments, or foreign sources. Documentary study is an essential activity for all historians, but it is not textual study. In textual study there is "no unseemly rush from word to world".[1] A body of writing, treated as a text, refers us to its language and not to outside events.

I mentioned de Saussure when I discussed what happened to Sanskrit loan words as evidence of the influence of language diversity. The focus in textual study owes much to de Saussure's insistence that a language is a system of relations between its constituent units, or between its words and combinations of words, and that all linguistic units are marked by relationships and differences among themselves.[2] Linguistic relations and differences provide the conditions which permit meaning to be produced. Figurative language, with its opportunities for options of meaning, feeds on linguistic relations and differences, and textual study pays particular heed to it. The study of a text, it has been said, is concerned "not with content, but with the process by which content is formulated".[3]

---

1. Jonathan Culler, *Structuralist Poetics, Structuralism, Linguistics, and the Study of Literature,* p. 130.
2. The following works provide a helpful introduction to de Saussure's theory of language: Jonathan Culler, *Saussure,* second impression (Fontana Modern Masters; Fontana Paperback, 1979); John Sturrock, ed., *Structuralism and Since. From Lévi-Strauss to Derrida* (Oxford University Press, 1979), pp. 6–10; and Terence Hawkes, *Structuralism and Semiotics* (University of California Press, 1977), pp. 19–28.
3. Terence Hawkes, op. cit., p. 158.

A crucial focus in this line of enquiry with special relevance for the study of the earlier Southeast Asian literatures is the investigation of what Jonathan Culler calls "literary conventions", shared by writers and readers alike within a particular culture. Conventions supply expectations of how meaning can be produced and communicated by literary effects. Culler defines "conventions" as "shared knowledge which would be recognized by participants as part of culture ...",[4] and he approvingly quotes Gérard Genette's statement: conventions are "a body of maxims and prejudices which constitute both a vision of the world and a system of values".[5] The vision and values, according to Culler, are what a text assumes as "natural" within its culture.[6] Or again, one reads a text as "the exploration of writing, or problems of articulating a world".[7] I approached the Angkor Wat monument on these lines.

This mode of literary study is clearly and firmly placed within the orbit of cultural studies. Literary conventions are a window through which the local ambience of writers and readers in a particular Southeast Asian subregion can be glimpsed; we are glimpsing something local people could not disregard. Culler's term for a community of literary conventions is "literary competence". The historian is invited to consider how and why language could formulate literary meaning in various parts of the region and in what ways formulations differed. Manifestations of literary competence within a culture seem to be akin to what Quaritch Wales calls "local genius" in the field of monumental art, and they may be a more satisfactory object of study because in language nothing can be isolated; everything is interrelated.

Textual study is not a branch of intellectual history and therefore another kind of sequential historical enquiry directly concerned with the study of ideas. Textual study remains committed to the study of the use of language and can be regarded as intellectual history only in so far as it deals with activities of the mind when the mind is engaged in literary production. Some may suppose that I am invoking an austere approach to the study of literature, which, as Culler puts it, discourages the reader from yielding to the "adventures of his own subjectivity", though in the Southeast Asian field tormenting problems of translation require most of us to postpone this kind of pleasure indefinitely. On the other hand, textual analysis can bring historians increments of new knowledge. By examining "literariness", the his-

4. Culler, *Structuralist Poetics*, p. 140.
5. Ibid., p. 144
6. Ibid., p. 144
7. Ibid., p. 260.

torian develops perspectives inaccessible to those accustomed to regard everything written as having documentary significance or nothing at all and do not consider what a text's language formulations can tell them.

Moreover, textual studies have already provided several insights for monitoring changes during more recent Southeast Asian history, and change is something that interests all historians. James Siegel points out a consequence of Muslim influence in Aceh, and therefore of cultural change: the *ulamas* insisted on the presence of a message in texts, whereas the epic tradition, studied by Siegel in great detail, was that sense was suppressed in favour of the sounds of the voice. Authority, according to the *ulamas*, stemmed from the substance of what was said and done.[8] Anthony Day, studying literary language in Central Java during the nineteenth century, isolates the time when the Javanese began to recognize and accept the impotence of kingship, which was after the Dipanegara war of 1830. But he rejects the view that post-1830 literature was "Byzantine", or involuted, and shows that the ancient poetic tradition of literary embellishment continued to produce creative writing, even though poetic language was now being used to render the end of Javanese kingship in Central Java. Benedict Anderson analyses the language of Sutomo's *Memories*. The author, founder of the Budi Utomo in 1908, does not describe his political life but rather how he discovered his Javanese cultural ancestry at the beginning of this century. The *Memories* end when Sutomo is nineteen and the Budi Utomo still unformed. Sutomo turns from Dutch or Indonesian to Javanese to express the nuances of his feelings, and episodes in his youth are often filled with sounds, not words. In spite of what has been subsequently written about Budi Utomo as marking the passage from "darkness to light", this imagery does not appear in *Memories*. Sutomo remembers change in his early life as the process of growing up by growing back. The language for describing the experience of meeting Dr Wahidin in 1907 expresses the completion of the process of becoming aware of a Javanese ancestry: a moral purpose in life was now revealed to the author and also the possibility of setting an example of Javanese excellence in the modern world without having to imitate the West.[9]

These three studies, to which I have not done justice, are based on careful examination of language. Unsuspected cultural changes are discovered, but change is never straightforward and obvious.

---

8. James Siegel, *Shadow and Sound. The Historical Thought of a Sumatran People*.
9. A.J. Day, "Meanings of Change in the Poetry of Nineteenth-Century Java"; B. Anderson, "A Time of Darkness and a Time of Light ...", *Perceptions of the Past in Southeast Asia*, pp. 219–48.

Though the type of textual study I have been sketching in a rudimentary fashion should not be expected to offer rule-of-thumb procedures for unearthing meaning in texts, the literatures of earlier Southeast Asia are a promising field for experimentation. Most literary materials are anonymous, so that one does not need to be distracted by questions about a writer's situation or personal intentions. One does not immediately have to look outside the texts to account for what is inside. Instead, one has to learn to read groups of texts in the same culture and genre to discern the presence of a local social collectivity which is expressing itself in language usage. Textual studies can also highlight something which tends to be given short shrift in accounts of earlier Southeast Asia: elements of "strangeness" in the various cultures when compared with each other and with cultures in other parts of the world. Literary texts are bound to be "strange" because they depend on figurative language. Various forms of literary strangeness are part of the "ranges of experience" which need to be opened up to allow satisfactory general accounts of earlier Southeast Asia to be written.

My interest in the localizing processes to which foreign materials had to submit before they could belong to cultural statements has led me to a particular approach to the phenomenon of cultural diversity: the study of language usages in local literatures. Documentary evidence points to something else outside itself, but foreign materials point to something else inside the local cultural statement, and the statement that now interests me is the text where foreign materials are subsumed by literary competence within the culture in question. Literatures are one means of illuminating cultural diversity. Textual studies will not, of course, yield rapid results, and the present priority is more knowledge of literary competence in each of the subregional cultures so that one day the foundation will be laid for comparative literary studies.

I shall now try to practise in an experimental and elementary way what I have been preaching. I shall discuss two seemingly unpromising examples of texts in non-Southeast Asian written languages, namely, Vietnamese poetry written in Chinese during the fourteenth century, and Sanskrit inscriptions written during the reign of Yaśovarman (889-910), the founder of the first of the cities known as Angkor. Differences between Vietnamese and Cambodian literary traditions are not my immediate concern; I am more interested in indicating a few considerations when studying literature in terms of literary processes rather than contents. I have also included in Appendix C notes on studies of the Old-Javanese *kakawins* and the Malay *hikayats* by P.J. Zoetmulder and Shelly Errington respectively. Zoetmulder's *Kalangwan. A survey of Old Javanese literature* is a valuable contribution to our knowledge of one literary culture in earlier Southeast Asia, while Errington's article is a stimulating example of the direction textual study can take one. Both scholars have helped to make textual study less of a stranger in this field of history, and the reason I have relegated them to appendices is that I believe that I should practise what I preach rather than quote others.

When one studies fourteenth century Vietnamese poetry, a major difficulty immediately arises. Can we even refer to "Vietnamese" poetry at that time? Poetry always calls attention to itself through its special language, and these poems seem to be explicitly calling attention not only to the Chinese language in which they were written but also to the complex rules of what is known as T'ang "new-style" prosody, with elaborate rhyming devices, couplets of parallel verse, and much more.[10] A considerable body of this kind of poetry has survived even though the annals record that Vietnamese in the fourteenth century were also using a local script (*nôm*), based on Chinese characters, for poetic writing. Moreover, the poets did not hesitate to use conventional Chinese word-combinations. They used the Chinese poetic convention of writing about the landscape as though they were seeing a painting. They appropriated expressions made famous by Chinese poets and sometimes admiringly referred to their work. They also employed well-known themes in Chinese poetry. Trần Quang Triều, for example, had Tu Fu's poem in mind when he wrote on Ch'ang-an, the fallen T'ang capital.[11] Their poems seem to be so packed with the conventions and topics of Chinese poetry that they may sometimes be mistaken for the work of Chinese poets.

---

10. Some of these rules are noted in *The Heritage of Vietnamese Poetry,* edited and translated by Huỳnh Sanh Thông, p. xxvii. On Chinese verse, see Hans H. Frankel, "Classical Chinese", *Versification: major language types*, pp. 22–37.

11. Quang Triêu's first line reads: "the rivers and peaks survived but the ancient state was no more". Tu Fu's first line is similar. Tu Fu, writing shortly after Ch'ang-an fell, goes on to describe the unkempt spring vegetation and the sorrow of the flowers and birds. Quang Triều, writing from a great distance of time, responds by referring to the cypresses of the imperial graves and the burying of the rulers' ardour under the autumn vegetation. In his third line, Tu Fu writes of a startled bird "as if with the anguish of separation", while Quang Triều, in his fourth line, thinks of the butterfly (perhaps an echo of Chuang-tzǔ) flying away in autumn to extinction. Tu Fu's poem is in eight lines, but Quang Triều chose to make variations only on the first four lines. For Tu Fu's poem, see David Hawkes, *A little primer of Tu Fu*, pp. 45–48. For Quang Triều's poem, see *Toàn Việt thi lụ-c (TVTL)*, HM 3139 in the library of the Société Asiatique, Paris, and a copy of Lê Quý Dôn's collection of Vietnamese poetry, compiled in the eighteenth century, q. 2, pp. 12b-13a.

In spite of these similarities, however, Chinese poetic forms had been localized, and the success of the localization may itself be furnishing a local statement. I believe that the poets were deliberately proclaiming their mastery of Chinese poetry to demonstrate that their countryside lent itself as convincingly to the highest standards of Chinese-style poetry as the Chinese countryside did in the poems of the T'ang masters and their successors. And so Phạm Su-Mạnh, writing on the famous Báo Thiên pagoda which protected the country in difficult times, ends: "I come to soak my pen in ink to compose a special poem. For my pen I want the stream to serve as my inkwell".[12]

The poets were celebrating their landscape by adorning what they wrote with all the Chinese literary devices available to them. They may have seen themselves as subordinating Chinese poetic forms, for they were living in the century after the Vietnamese victories over the Mongols. Their poems would have been a gesture of homage all the more impressive because they were using the language which was the Chinese poets' preserve. Here may be an instance of poetic justice in the literal as well as in the figurative sense. Their behaviour could have been as combative as that of the historian in 1272, when he appropriated Chinese literary fragments to defend his ruler's independent status in the face of Chinese imperial pretensions.

Nevertheless, can poetry written in this style be regarded as Vietnamese poetry? One reason that the poems, in spite of their script, were Vietnamese and not Chinese is surely that they were vocalized in the local language. Scholars in the Hàn-lâm academy in Thăng-long could sometimes speak Chinese and were available for welcoming Northern envoys,[13] but one should not assume that all literati were similarly qualified. Trần Nhật Duật, who was conspicuous for his interest in foreign languages, picked up some facility in spoken Chinese by mingling with Chinese envoys in the thirteenth century,[14] but this does not mean that Vietnamese poets wrote with the Chinese sounds of the script in their ears; it is unthinkable that they did so when their poems named and celebrated the country's famous sites. The Chinese script had been used for administrative and educational purposes since the beginning of the Christian era and continued to be used for these purposes when the Vietnamese regained independence in the tenth century. The inevitable result

12. *Tho-văn Lý-Trần (TVLT)*, Nhà Xuất Bãn Khoa Học Xã Hội, vol. 3 (Hanoi, 1978), p. 115.
13. *TT* (the Vietnamese annals), under the date of 1324.
14. Ibid., under the date of 1330.

was that many Chinese words were assimilated over the centuries into the Vietnamese language. But the Chinese characters were always pronounced in Vietnamese, and the poets would have effortlessly converted the Chinese characters into Vietnamese sounds. Thus, when Nguyễn Phi Khanh wrote that "he will chant a [T'ang new style] poem to teach my young boy", he must have intended to chant in the Vietnamese language.[15] The emotive associations of Vietnamese speech-sounds and their relation to meaning are one of the many questions needing study before more is known about Vietnamese literature in the fourteenth century, but a safe assumption is that the poets sometimes chose particular Chinese characters for the sake of the sheer sound of the words when they were uttered in Vietnamese speech.[16] One should not forget that the development of the *nôm* script as a vehicle for poetry in the fourteenth century was precisely to provide a script that could be sounded in Vietnamese.

The poems are "Vietnamese" in a more recognizable way, though here, too, further study is needed. The poets appropriated Chinese written characters to create their own literary conventions. A straightforward instance is the language used to poeticize Tãn Viên, a famous mountain about sixty miles west of the capital city of Thăng-long on the site of Hanoi. "Tãn Viên" appears as a linguistic unit only three times in the "Chinese" poetry of the second half of the fourteenth century but always in a similar literary formulation. Phạm Su-Mạnh wrote:

> The blue sky over Tãn Viên shines down on Thang-long.[17]

And again,

> The appearance of the Tãn Viên mountain is clear to the ninth heaven.[18]

Another poet, the prince Phũ and future ruler Nghệ-tôn, presented a farewell poem to the first Ming envoy in 1369. He wrote:

> Annam's aged minister of state lacks the poet's skill.
> He only offers a cup of tea to bid his guest farewell.

---

15. *TVLT*, p. 395.
16. I am alluding to Edward Sapir's enthusiasm for the "wild joy in the *sheer sound* of words" which he found in the poetry of Gerard Manley Hopkins, and I owe the reference to Roman Jakobson and Linda R. Waugh, *The Sound Shape of Language*, p. 231. Chapter four ("The Spell of Speech Sounds") discusses research in this field of linguistics.
17. *TVLT*, p. 121. Tãn Viên's three peaks can be seen in the west from Hanoi in clear weather.
18. Ibid., p. 102.

> The Tãn Viên mountain is green. The Lô river is blue.
> May you have a favourable wind as you fly into the land of many-coloured clouds.[19]

Phũ intensifies the clear colours of the mountain and river by suggesting a contrast between them and the colours of the clouds awaiting the envoy in southern China. In these three poems Tãn Viên is always associated with fine weather, and the reason is that the poets are familiar with the folklore image of the mountain as the abode of the spirit who fights the rain spirit and protects the capital and rice plains from unseasonal flooding. The language used to adorn the mountain is a literary convention to signify the spirit's benign influence.

The Vietnamese also gave Chinese literary expressions nuances of their own. In Chinese literature "axles and script" is an equivalence of word "standardization" and a mark of ancient civilization in China, but in fourteenth-century Vietnamese poetry and prose the expression was used to refer to the glorious dawn of Vietnamese civilization in the first millennium BC. The nuance became conventional because "standardization" implied stable government, and those who used it were expressing their concern over the collapse of authority in their own day.[20]

"Axles and script" is a figure of speech, and all Chinese historical and literary allusions in fourteenth-century Vietnamese literature should normally be understood as being no more than literary devices, whether they appear in the always ornate language of poetry or in the often ornate language of Chinese prose. The writer's literary intentions have to be borne in mind to avoid misunderstanding what he means when he refers to Chinese philosophers or uses special Chinese vocabulary to refer to Chinese political and moral values and the institutions embodying them. This kind of material should, in the absence of convincing evidence to the contrary, be expected only to provide literary effects. The writers introduce figurative language even when they are referring to themselves; they are not announcing their allegiance to Chinese ideals. To approach Vietnamese decorative language otherwise is to run the risk of habitually looking for outside explanations of what was happening inside Vietnam. The Vietnamese writers' language can be likened to that of the

19. Ibid., p. 217.
20. I discuss this convention in "Assertions of Cultural Well-being in Fourteenth Century Vietnam: Part II", *JSEAS* 11, no. 1 (1980): 77–78. A poem by the fourteenth century official, Nguyễn Phi Khanh, contains the same convention; see *TVLT*, p. 453.

Javanese poets, who wrote about their countryside and society under the guise of Sanskrit personal and place names.

We have seen in the previous chapter that the Buddhist ruler Trần Thái-tôn presented himself as a Vietnamese version of the Chinese sage and ruler, Yao. He did so because Yao signified a prescient ruler, and Trần Nguyên Đán did likewise towards the end of the fourteenth century when he wrote in a poem: "it is easier to fly to Heaven in daytime than to serve a ruler such as Yao and Shun".[21] His poem is no more than an expression of hopelessness at a time when the ruler was incompetent. In happier times Đán had written a poem, packed with Chinese imagery, to show his admiration for the famous fourteenth-century scholar, Chu Văn An.[22] The language evokes the image of Han Yü, the highly motivated and irascible late T'ang Confucianist who wanted to revive the teachings of the ancient philosophers at the expense of Buddhism. But, although in Đán's day Vietnamese monks, breaking free from their monastic discipline, were persuading villagers to join bands of armed peasants, Đán's poem was not intended to ascribe Han Yü's political philosophy to Chu Văn An. The latter is characterized in the annals as capable of anger when confronted by stupid students or corrupt officials, and Đán is using hyperbolic language only because he wants to metaphorize his hero by likening the impression An made to the impression made by the indignant Han Yü. Đán was giving literary force to his praise, just as Lý Nhân-tôn did when he enclosed his death-bed edict within the text of a Han emperor's edict. Both Đán and Nhân-tôn wanted to make their points as effectively as possible.

These poems must be read cautiously before one decides that they provide evidence of Confucianist influence and not simply of the poets' familiarity with Chinese materials for producing literary effects. The language is always that of poetry, and poetic language is liable to supply misleading information when read for documentary purposes. Nevertheless, the poems yield their own kind of information. Tãn Viên's bright sky and "axles and script" are opportunities for discovering the assumptions concealed by local conventions.

But poetry can reveal more than conventional language usage if we remember the essential question to be put to a "text": how is its

21. *TVLT*, p. 207.
22. The poem is translated in Huỳnh Sanh Thông, *The Heritage of Vietnamese Poetry*, p. 31, no. 75. For a translation of the first four lines, see O.W. Wolters, "Assertions of Cultural Well-being in Fourteenth Century Vietnam: Part I", *JSEAS* 10, no. 2 (1979): 448.

content formulated by the use of language? To suggest what is possible, I shall make a few comments on Vietnamese landscape poetry in the second half of the fourteenth century.

When poets wrote about the landscape, they sometimes used the phrase "the mountains and the rivers". This is another Chinese expression and means "territory", but it refers to the territory identified in the annals as "our Đại Việt", or "our Vietnam". The local identity of "the mountains and rivers" is guaranteed by the frequent contiguity of two other words: "barrier" and "since antiquity". The literary association of "territory" therefore signify successful and timeless protection provided by "the mountains and rivers". The ruler Minh-tôn (1300-57) in a poem about Bạch Đằng, where the Mongols were defeated for the final time in 1288, poeticizes the landscape in military equivalences and, in his second couplet in parallel verse, writes:

> The mountains and rivers have been here since antiquity.
> They open their eyes in both directions.
> The Mongols and Vietnamese, defeat and victory. Both depended on [natural] barriers.[23]

The poets sometimes enlarge the associations of mountains and rivers to include heroism. For example, Nguyễn Su-o-ng writes about the Bạch Đằng victory:

> Who could have known that this enduring achievement [in the 1285-1293 reign-period]
> Depended equally on the barrier river and on men?[24]

Vietnam's capacity for surviving required language of its own.

The Vietnamese landscape could also be contrasted with that on the other side of the northern border. To leave Vietnam on a diplomatic mission to the North required an elaborate language of dark and cold mountains, damp and unhealthy vapours, crude mountain settlements, and "screaming monkeys". Nguyễn Su-o-ng said of the envoy, Nguyễn Trung Ngạn:

> You are following the geese across the mountain passes to face the northern snow.
> But your heart is that of the Vietnamese bird longing for its southern branch.[25]

---

23. *TVLT*, q. 1, pp. 20b–21a. Some of the river stakes on which the Mongols' evacuation fleet was impaled at low tide are on display in the National Museum, Hanoi.
24. *TVTL*, q. 2, p. 15b.
25. *TVTL*, q. 2, p. 14b. Su-o-ng is celebrating the Bạch Đằng victory.

"The Vietnamese bird" is the peacock, whose harsh cry was a Chinese metaphor for nostalgia.[26] Su-o-ng appropriates the Chinese use of the metaphor as a means of honouring his own country; Ngạn is going into temporary exile. Ngạn, a prolific poet, upsets the meaning of a Chinese poem when he borrows from Li Po the expression "it is better to go home" to refer to his unhappiness when he is on a mission to China.

> Although Jiang-nan (southern China) is a happy place, it is better to go home.[27]

The theme of exile may draw on Chinese poetry referring to service on the frontier but the land of exile is China.

Vietnamese poems about "the mountains and rivers" have provided some examples of local poetic conventions. Equivalences of defence, timelessness, physical discomfort in southern China, and homesickness belong to Vietnamese literary competence. But the language of landscape poetry written in the second half of the fourteenth century can tell us something more about literary formulation at that time. About fifteen poems by three prominent poets reveal a textual structure for articulating the experience of wandering in beautiful scenery.[28] These poems continue to include conventional elements in Chinese poetry, especially the way in which natural scenery, represented as the threshold of the supernatural world, becomes an escape from the pressures of daily life. Nevertheless, features of the language usage are Vietnamese.

The structure of the poems is revealed in the thematic similarities in each of the corresponding couplets. Some poems have four couplets, while the structure of those with only two couplets seems to correspond with that of the third and fourth couplets in the long poems. Although the poet conforms to the structure, he treats it in his own way. When a poem has four couplets, the first one situates the poet among the mountains. Sometimes he may note a cliff "thrusting itself into the blue heavens like a jade lotus" or that "a tall bamboo on the

---

26. Edward H. Schafer, *The Vermilion Bird. T'ang images of the South*, p. 237.
27. *TVTL*, q. 2, pp. 40a-b. Bùi Bích, an eighteenth-century compiler of Vietnamese poetry, observes that Ngạn, in his preceding line, adapts a line from a T'ang poet, Shu Yu, when he writes: "It is said that, in one's own family, even poverty is good"; see Bùi Bích, *Hoàng Việt thi tuyển*, q. 2, p. 8a.
28. I have translated seven of Phạm Su-Mạnh's poems in "Phạm Su-Mạnh's poems written when patrolling the Vietnamese northern border in the middle of the fourteenth century", *JSEAS* (in press). Number IV of these poems ("The Tam Thanh grotto") can also be grouped among the poems discussed below. See Appendix B for translations of six of these poems.

mountain top pierces through the cloud mist".[29] A poet may be leading a military patrol in the northern provinces, in which case his first couplet will convey the effects of bustle and movement, set in train by the ruler's orders.[30] Or again, he may be snatching a moment's leisure from his official duties, and this will enable him to contrast the affairs of the world with nature's solitude.[31] The weather is always fine, and the poet can survey limitless space. Exciting scenery must be spacious.

The second couplets are in parallel verse and deliberately decorative in language. Poems written on patrol may allude to peaks and streams in the contorted landscape or may flourish flags, horses, and soldiers to convey the sensation of military influences operating in the scene.[32] In poems written at leisure, another kind of influence is at work. The poets sometimes hear the sounds of nature or see a spirit-fashioned palace in the white clouds. In several poems they even glimpse the abode of immortal spirits through the distant haze, and they intensify the sensation of spiritual presence by alluding to descriptions in Chinese literature of the spirits' magical islands in the North China Sea.[33] The effect conveyed in second couplets is always that fine scenery becomes privileged scenery.

The third couplets, again in parallel verse, reveal that the influences referred to in the second couplets are actually occupying the scene. When poems are written on patrol, we read of "cavalry" and "brave troops" or of defensive points in the mountains and passes.[34] The theme of occupation is maintained in poems where spiritual influences appear in the second couplets. Spirit imagery may extend into the third couplets, or a poet may announce that he, too, has become a spirit.[35] Illustrious Vietnamese place-names can also emerge in the enchanted scene as a matter of course. The first line in a two-couplet poem mentions "the mountains and rivers" of Tiên Du, the ancestral home of the Lý dynasty, and goes on to compare the scene with one of the spirits' islands.[36] A third couplet in another poem mentions Vạn Kiếp with its "rows of chilled halberds".[37] Vạn

29. Poem 4 in Appendix B.
30. See Phạm Su-Mạnh's poems in *JSEAS* (in press).
31. Poems 1, 2, and 4 in Appendix B.
32. See Phạm Su-Mạnh's poems in *JSEAS* (in press.)
33. Poems 1, 2, 3, 5 and 6 in Appendix B. The islands' location is described in the *Ch'ien Han-shu, chiao-szǔ chih*.
34. See Phạm Su-Mạnh's poems in *JSEAS* (in press).
35. Poems 1 and 4 in Appendix B.
36. Poem 5 in Appendix B.
37. Poem 3 in Appendix B.

Kiếp was a battlefield in the Mongol wars and the fief of the famous commander-in-chief, the Hu-ng-đạo prince. Another third couplet mentions Bạch-Đằng, where the final victory took place in 1288. The poet wrote:

> The world's most marvellous sight is the rising of the sun at
> Du-o-ng Cốc.
> The purest air of the rivers and mountains is Bạch-Đằng's
> autumn.[38]

Du-o-ng Cốc, "the bright valley", was the place designated by the Chinese sage and ruler Yao for announcing the beginning of spring activities by the rising sun. The passage is from the Chinese classic *The Book of History* and the reference permits the poet to emphasize the unique atmosphere of this honoured part of the Vietnamese countryside.

The final couplet in each poem describes the poet's elation. He is carefree, sings and plays music, writes a poem, or rejoices in the invigorating air. He has put the world behind him. One poet observes that the spirits do not concern themselves with the past; they are in a realm where time is of no account.

The adoption of this basic structure leaves the poets free to concentrate on the use of poetic language. Peaks, grottos, mist, magical music, air, and, above all, spaciousness call for good poetry. Humans are consigned to the distant hurly-burly of public life unless they are soldiers on duty, a solitary monk in his mountain retreat, or the excited poet. Peaks, mist, and so forth help to signify the space, mystery, and timelessness of "the mountains and rivers". We seem to be dealing with sets of signifying associations that link the poets with their readers in a cultural transaction. The poets knew that their readers would read these poems as expressions of elation, and the language of elation is associated with "mountains and rivers", together with "barrier", "since antiquity", and "heroism".

The structure and much of the language of these poems could have originated from Chinese poetry. What is interesting about them and gives them the texture of poetry written in the second half of the fourteenth century is the allusions to the distant islands of the spirits. Several islands are mentioned: Bồng Lai (P'eng-lai in Chinese), Phu-o-ng Hồ (Fang-hu), Doanh Châu (Ting-chọu), and Viên Kiệu (Yuan-ch'iao). These magical place-names do not appear in the

38. Poem 2 in Appendix B.

poetry of the first half of the century,[39] but in the second half of the century no less than four islands are localized by three prominent poets among the "mountains and rivers" of Vietnam. A new literary convention suddenly appears, and the interest of the innovation is enhanced when we bear in mind that other literary changes also appear in the same vintage of poems. "Axles and script" and "Văn Lang", the site of Vietnam's golden age, appear in a poem by Phạm Su-Manh, who wrote of Vạn Kiêp and Bạch-Đăng in his poems of elation.[40] Moreover, even a cursory glance at the poems of the later fourteenth century shows that writers were drawing on a much wider range of Chinese literary allusions for metaphorizing the trials and tribulations of public life.

How should these literary changes be explained? The annals make it painfully clear that the Trần dynasty was being threatened by an usurper at a time when there was grave social unrest and the borders were defenceless. The poets were also officials deeply involved in the deteriorating situation. Moreover, although their traditional role had been that of court "servants", they were now becoming the unhappy monitors of public life.[41] It is not surprising that they would steal some moments of leisure amid beautiful scenery, but their preoccupations accompanied them. What, then, does their poetic language tell us? The poems, and especially the allusions to the magical islands they fancied that they could see in the distance in order to highlight their elation, call attention to the special quality of the Vietnamese landscape – its timelessness and, by implication, capacity for enduring. The language of timelessness is conveyed by soldiers on the barrier passes and especially by the novel language of spiritual influences, metaphorized by the immortal spirits. Poetry provides the opportunity for these writers to celebrate their country's most precious quality. They were as concerned with poetical processes as the Javanese poets were (see Appendix C), but their purpose was to salute "our Đại Việt". Fine scenery elated them because it reminded them that the ancient "mountains and rivers" were now the single stable landmark in dangerous times. If we suppose that the Old-Javanese poems are our means of participating in yogic meditation, the happening in these Vietnamese poems is the poets' replenishment of hope for the future.

39. See Nguyễn Ú-c, *TVLT*, p. 45. A variant reading of this poem gives Bồng Lai, but the editors of *TVLT* have properly preferred Bồng Vân, the name of a Trần palace.

40. See Phạm Su-Mạnh's poem no. vii in *JSEAS* (in press). On Văn Lang, see O.W. Wolters, "Assertions of Cultural Well-being: Part II", pp. 74–78.

41. Ibid., pp. 84–87.

I shall now leave Vietnam in order to consider Yaśovarman I's inscriptions, written in Cambodia towards the end of the ninth century or in the first years of the tenth. I am not attempting to compare Vietnamese and Cambodian literatures. I am only suggesting another possibility for studying literature elsewhere in earlier Southeast Asia. The undertaking is risky, for I shall be trespassing on the Sanskritists' preserve.

Yaśovarman I's inscriptions and many others before and during Angkorian times are all that survive of earlier Cambodian literature. The poems are packed with allusions to the same Hindu deities who appear in the Javanese *kakawins*, studied by Zoetmulder, but this does not necessarily mean that there were few differences between the two literatures. Indeed, in one respect the Cambodian inscriptions resemble the Vietnamese poems, for they were also written in a foreign language, Sanskrit, and those who study them insist that the poets were familiar with the prosody of Indian *kāvya* literature, with its highly organized forms, figurative language, and richness of metres, all of which were "aimed at producing methodically a defined aesthetic experience in an audience, hearer, or reader".[42] The Vietnamese poets refer admiringly to Chinese poetry and, I believe, expected their own poems to be judged by the standards of excellence found in the best Chinese poetry. Likewise, the Cambodian inscriptions praise rulers and scholars for having an expert knowledge of the Sanskrit language and literature.[43] Just as Chinese literary forms did not stifle Vietnamese poets, so Sanskrit literary forms need not have done so in Cambodia.

The Sanskrit inscriptions of Cambodia, as far as I know, are not usually studied as "texts". The literary feature that catches their editors' attention is an apparently suffocating profusion of Indian materials used for eulogizing gods and rulers. The inscriptions of the later ninth century have been described as "over-refined"[44] and showing a propensity for "repetition" not common in India.[45] Coedès observes that the use of "decoration" (*alaṃkāra*) in some twelfth-century inscriptions exceeds the worst that the preceding centuries had produced. Of an early twelfth-century inscription he says that it exceeds in silliness the worst that the poets of the Angkor court had produced.[46] But we need not take his criticisms too

42. A.K. Warder, "Classical Literature", *A Cultural History of India*, p. 171.
43. For example, see A. Barth and A. Bergaigne, *ISCC*, p. 522, v. 1.
44. Ibid., p. 335.
45. Ibid., p. 347.
46. Coedès, *IC*,, vol. 4, p. 208; *IC*, vol. 6, p. 301. Coedès notes an instance of gibberish; *IC*, vol. 3, p. 108, note 1.

seriously. De Casparis writes about an excessive use of "decoration" in an Old-Javanese inscription of 856, and he is identifying a distinctive feature of creative writing found in Java during the following thousand years.[47] Nevertheless, the usual judgment passed on the poetic quality of the Cambodian inscriptions may have discouraged historians from searching them for more than documentary evidence.

Not all, however, have read the inscriptions in this way. Mabbett's essay on the "Devarāja", where he develops Jean Filliozat's views, is an important exception.[48] Filliozat insists that the poets were less intent on praising a king than on establishing his identification with divine models. "What is at stake is not royal vanity but the transference to the kingdom of sovereignty over the universe, a transference which the panegyrist does more than record — which he consecrates and reconsecrates in his poetic formula, even as the architect gives it effect in the symbolic monuments.... When the Sanskrit poets [in India and so in Cambodia] equate kings with gods ... they compose in a medium where gods are not simply literary themes but basically sovereign realities ...."[49] In Mabbett's words, we are dealing with parts of an exercise "conducted according to a single set of rules to assimilate the kingdom to the heavens and thereby allow divinity to flow down. The exercise required the establishment in various ways of the equivalence of a king to a god".[50]

Mabbett goes on to suggest that the language of Khmer religious symbols, including that of the inscriptions, should be regarded as "the language of a society, employed to formulate ideas that were important to that society, rather than as the propaganda of a succession of megalomaniacs".[51] The symbols, "like words in a language", are manipulated to make statements. That the symbols are equivalent to the things they represent "is not itself a statement in the language; it is an initial convention that is necessary before any statement can be made."[52] This last point seems to be critically important for understanding Sanskrit inscriptions in Cambodia.

Filliozat and Mabbett, when they read the inscriptions, recognize them as literary texts, replete with devices for literary

47. See Appendix C.
48. I.W. Mabbett, "Devarāja", *JSEAS* 10, no. 2 (1969); 202–23.
49. Ibid., pp. 219–20. He is quoting Filliozat, "Le Symbolisme du Monument de Phnom Bakheng", *BEFEO* 44, no. 2 (1954): 549 f.
50. Mabbett, op. cit., p. 220.
51. Ibid., p. 221.
52. Ibid., p. 221.

statements about "the basic truths of the universe".[53] Mabbett's views are consistent with the approach to literature that I have been discussing. He does not hesitate to speak of "a society", "formulation", "equivalence", "convention", and "statement", and the result is that he throws the possibility wide open for textual study by Sanskritists.[54]

By way of hypothesis, I shall suggest a specific sub-study. Even those whose access to the inscriptions is limited to translations cannot fail to observe that certain words appear time and time again. Perhaps the meanings of some of these words were conventionally interrelated and represented a set of signifying language associations familiar to the Khmer poets. One such set may appear in Yaśovarman's inscriptions.

A verse purports to state the king's intention when he constructed the Yaśodharataṭāka lake to the east of his new city. Its name is derived from the king's name, *Yaśas*, meaning "glory". We are told that the king wanted to "facilitate an outlet for his abundant glory (*yaśas*) in the direction of the underworld (*rasātala*)".[55] The "underworld" is the abode of the *nāgas*, aquatic and serpentine creatures associated with the soil's riches. Another inscription connects "glory" with the lake and also provides a metaphor for the lake. The king, "resplendent with glory", has built the lake, "beautiful as the moon to refresh human beings".[56] In Indian imagery, the moon teems with life-sustaining ambrosia (*amṛita*), and one of the king's inscriptions follows the convention: he has constructed a lake "equal to the disc of the moon and whose substance could come from water" and be precipitated on the earth.[57] The editor glosses the passage as meaning "whose *amṛita* could come from water".[58]

53. Ibid., p. 222.
54. Louis Renou, in a study of the structure of the Indian *kāvya*, describes the ornate features of the autonomous strophes such as *double entendre*, synonyms, and by no means always self-evident comparisons, sometimes based on comparisons with grammatical analogies. He suggests that insufficient attention has been paid to "form" in Indian poetry, where form takes precedence over content. By "form", he is not thinking of grammatical categories but of "structure", which is the point where morphological questions come to an end and the "meaning" (*valeur*) of the style or structure begins. "Formalisme" would be a rewarding field for Indian literary studies; see Louis Renou, "Sur la structure de kāvya", *Journal Asiatique* 247, no. 1 (1959): 61.
55. A. Barth and A. Bergaigne, op. cit., p. 407, v. 54.
56. Ibid., p. 473, v. 22.
57. Ibid., p. 502, v. 22.
58. Ibid., p. 502, note 5.

The relationship between royal glory and ambrosia, implied in these references to the lake, is made explicit in other inscriptions of the reign. "He spreads everywhere and ceaselessly the *amṛita* (ambrosia) of his immaculate glory".[59] Or again, the king's glory is likened to a lotus stalk.[60] The lotus, and especially its stalk, has a special significance in Indian mythology. The god Brahmā, the Indian god of creation, was born in a lotus (growing from Viṣṇu's navel), and the lotus became an Indian metaphor for the created world; in Bosch's words, it is "the very symbol of life risen from the waters".[61] Thus, one inscription compares the lake with "the lotus where the creator is born".[62] In Indian mythology, the waters where the lotus floats came to be associated with the life-sustaining substance known as the germ of life or *amṛita* (ambrosia). The precious substance was released when the creator married Vāc ("Voice"), the goddess of the waters.[63] Vāc became the god's *śakti*, activator of his creative energy, and the lotus stalk, because it was absorbing Vāc's water, was regarded as signifying the essence of the germ of life, or ambrosia, which supported life in the newly created world. The statement that Yaśovarman's glory was to be compared with a lotus stalk is attributing to him the life-sustaining energy released when the creator married Vāc.

The lake, in poetic language, is a receptacle for the king's glory, which is his store of ambrosia. The relationship between the king and ambrosia is expressed even more strikingly. The royal voice is also associated with ambrosia. It is said that from Yaśovarman's mouth went out only "the ambrosia of his commands (*sāsanāmṛita*) for the prosperity of his subjects".[64] The water of his commands "purified the hearts" of the defiled.[65] Or again, one drank "the *amṛita* of his voice".[66]

We must now return to Indian mythology to understand the reason. When Vāc became the creator's consort, the germ of life possessed her and she began to speak. Speech was thus instituted at the moment of creation, when ambrosia was released. Because the origins of ambrosia and speech were coeval, speech was associated with the mediation of ambrosia and was therefore a purifying in-

59. Ibid., p. 426, v. 7.
60. Ibid., p. 466, v. 11.
61. F.D.K. Bosch, *The Golden Germ. An Introduction to Indian Symbolism*, p. 82.
62. A. Barth and A. Bergaigne, op. cit., p. 525, v. 22.
63. On Vāc, see Bosch, *The Golden Germ*, p. 53.
64. A. Barth and A. Bergaigne, op. cit., p. 440, v. 20.
65. Ibid., p. 427, v. 14.
66. Ibid., p. 519, v. 4.

fluence. The purifying influence of Vāc's speech is eulogised in an early tenth-century inscription written not long after Yaśovarman's death, and the association would be known when the king's inscriptions were being composed.[67] Vāc, and also the king, release ambrosia when they speak, and this equivalence in speech strengthens the impression that the poets wished to portray the king as the source of life-sustaining energy.

The royal voice is sometimes metaphorized as the goddess Sarasvatī, another name for Vāc (Vagīśwarī). Sarasvatī is said to have "resided in" a king's mouth.[68] She is Brahmā's consort and honoured in India and Southeast Asia as the goddess of eloquence, writing, and music, though Zoetmulder remarks that she was much less prominent in the invocations (*manggalas*) at the beginning of the Old-Javanese *kakawins* than she became in Bali.[69] In Angkorian Cambodia more respect seems to have been paid to Sarasvatī than to her consort, and, as in India, she was also identified as the consort of Śiva or Viṣṇu.[70] A tenth-century inscription states that Vagīswarī (Vāc) was Śiva's *śakti*,[71] and an early eleventh-century one records sacrifices to Śiva and Sarasvatī.[72]

The lake, linked with ambrosia-charged royal glory, therefore provides an opportunity for the poets to use the language of divine kingship when they are writing about their ruler. Divinity flows down from the heavens to permeate the king, and the effect is achieved by a cluster of related words which endow him with the capacity of dispensing and even voicing purifying ambrosia. The effect is possible because the Khmer poets were familiar with the Indian imagery of ambrosia as a result of their own literary competence. The poets' readers would know that the king was being described as a god with creative energy. Who, then, is the creator god who has descended to earth?

The inscriptions unambiguously identify Brahmā, Vāc's husband, as the god of creation. He is referred to when the lake is compared with "the lotus where the creator is born", and Cambodian epigraphy from the seventh century onwards leaves us in no doubt that Brahmā was honoured in this way. But in India, and also in Southeast Asia, Śiva's worshippers considered Brahmā as one of Śiva's manifestations, and the same relationship between the two gods is an-

67. Coedès, *IC*, vol. 3, p. 108, v. 10.
68. Ibid., p. 226, v. 3.
69. P.J. Zoetmulder, *Kalangwan*, p. 174.
70. K. Bhattacharya, *Les Religions Brahmaniques dans l' Ancien Cambodge*, p. 127.
71. Coedès, *IC*, vol. 4, p. 139, v. 1.
72. K. Bhattacharya, op. cit., p. 127.

nounced in invocations at the beginning of these inscriptions.[73] Thus, for them Śiva, and not Brahmā, is the creator god. During the king's lifetime Śiva was in "his heart", and to listen to his words was to hear "the mysterious words of Śiva".[74] When Yaśovarman died, he was described as having gone to Śiva's abode (*Paramaśivaloka*). The king's creative energy was certainly conceptualized as Śiva's, and nowhere is the model of the king's divine authority more confidently expressed than in the following passage:

> The creator is astonished and seems to say to himself: why then have I created for myself a rival in this king who is another Prajāpati (a name for Brahmā) and, moreover, why have I made a Parameśvara (Śiva)?[75]

As the editor explains, the creator, Brahmā, finds that he has created a being not only equal to him but also to Śiva and, as a result, superior to himself.[76]

These poets are using Sanskrit language worthy of a king whom they wish, though never explicitly, to associate with Śiva's authority on earth and to whom they are transferring the god's creative and purifying energy. The poets are not depicting royal creativity in figurative speech but are consecrating Yaśovarman with his own appropriate language in order to make their statement about the universe, which is the equivalence of Cambodia. To read of the king is to read of Śiva, and vice versa. The clearest expression of the poets' statement is that "he spreads everywhere and ceaselessly the *amṛita* of his immaculate glory". In this passage the king is allowed to stand alone without being metaphorized as an Indian god. He is not "like" Śiva but is Śiva-like. The passage stating that from his mouth went out only "the ambrosia of his commands" is similarly unadorned by metaphor; in fact, metaphor has been specifically rejected in the immediately preceding lines: "From the mouth of Prajāpati (Brahmā) went out formerly [here are illegible words] destroyers of the creatures, but from his mouth [the king's] went out only the ambrosia of his commands".

This brief discussion began with the verse that refers to the release of royal glory in the direction of the "underworld", and I conclude that the verse means no more than that the royal ambrosia was reaching the world of the *nāgas* beneath the soil. The passage appears

73. For example, see A. Barth and A. Bergaigne, op. cit., p. 402, verses 1–2, and note 7; p. 487, v. 3.
74. Ibid., p. 451, v. 14.
75. Ibid., p. 372, v. 26.
76. Ibid., p. 372, note 4.

naturally after a verse in honour of the king's military prowess and is equally naturally followed by a verse that compares his glory with that of the Indian epic hero Arjuna and his impetuosity with that of Bhīma, another epic hero.[77] The lake is intended to provide a further instance of the same glory.[78]

I have reached this conclusion after trying to recover the literary function of a particular cluster of words. The words seem to belong to the conventional language of the poets, but the statement they wished to formulate is not less important for that reason. They were formulating the meaning of royal authority at the beginning of the Angkorian period; the king was the source of creative and life-sustaining authority in Cambodia. The statement is as massively decked with localized Indian literary materials as Angkor Wat's statement about the privilege of living in Sūryavarman II's generation more than two centuries later. The inscriptions and the great monument seem to illustrate Mabbett's view that Indian symbols or, as I prefer to call them, "signifiers", were being employed in this society to express important local ideas.

Sanskritists would be able to undertake informed textual studies not only of Yaśovarman's inscriptions but also of those in earlier and later times, and new information on shifts in literary formulations might be discovered and be of general historical interest. How, for example, would a tenth-century Khmer account for every verse and trope in a long Sanskrit inscription in order to understand the force of its language, and would a twelfth-century Khmer have to be familiar with different conventions in order to read an inscription composed in his lifetime? My impression is that seventh-century inscriptions do not resemble Yaśovarman's even though they are in Sanskrit. Brahmā honours Śiva,[79] and Bhāratī (another name for Sarasvatī) is in an overlord's mouth,[80] but the prominent cluster of words concerns "asceticism". Royal glory is inevitably eulogised, but in military terms and not in terms of "ambrosia" and "purification". I have

77. Ibid., p. 407, v. 55.
78. I had always assumed that this and other artificial lakes in the Angkor complex were also connected with the irrigation of rice-fields in the neighbourhood of Angkor. Van Liere's examination of the site contradicts this view. Nowhere are the temple-ponds or city moats equipped with distribution systems to water the surrounding rice-fields. Indeed, what he calls "theocratic hydraulic works" impeded drainage. The conclusion of his study is that "the service of the Gods had much higher priority than the service of man"; see W.J. van Liere, "Traditional water management in the lower Mekong Basin", *World Archaeology* 11, no. 3 (1980): 265–80.
79. A. Barth and A. Bergaigne, op. cit., p. 68, v. 1.
80. Ibid., p. 20, v. 2.

found no reference to "ambrosia" in the seventh-century inscriptions.

Sacral language may have been different in the ninth century because new ideas, requiring new literary conventions, were in the air, as they were in Vietnam during the second half of the fourteenth century. We should not forget that the ninth century began with Jayavarman II's famous religious ceremony on Mount Mahendra in 802. Scholars have generally supposed that Śaivite tantric texts, known in India, were used to inaugurate the king's personal cult, the *devarāja* (the cult of "the king of the gods", who is Śiva).[81] Tantric texts, by definition, provide initiation rituals for reproducing divine powers in the initiate, and the ritual on Mount Mahendra was said in an inscription of 1052 to be based on a "procedure" (*sādhana*) for bringing about "success" (*siddhi*). These words form the basis of tantric rituals. If I am correct in believing that the great conqueror Jayavarman II had established new criteria for kingly leadership in Khmer society, new rituals could have been required for identifying this remarkable man of prowess with divinity. The belief that the king was the most successful practitioner of asceticism was sufficient in the seventh century but not in the wake of Jayavarman's feats, and new religious rites and also new sacral language could have been necessary. Sacral language with tantric significance was being used in central Java in the ninth century,[82] and there is no reason that it should not have been used in ninth-century Cambodia. The localization of tantrism, Śaivite and Mahāyāna, in different parts of Southeast Asia could provide one framework for periodizing earlier history in the region.

Tantric initiation ceremonies can involve ritual consorts, and later Sanskrit inscriptions refer to royal marriages of no ordinary kind. At the end of the twelfth century the king, presumably Jayavarman VII, is said to have married the city of Yaśodharapurī (Angkor) for "the procreation of the good fortune of the universe".[83] Again, a thirteenth-century inscription refers to the union of the Earth and "the ardent vital principle of the king which produces numerous riches".[84] The metaphor of conjugal relations between the king and the Earth is also found in Indian literature,[85] and the Cambodian

81. George Coedès, *The Indianized States of Southeast Asia,* p. 101.
82. J.G. de Casparis, *Prasasti Indonesia II,* 266, 275.
83. George Coedès, *IC,* vol. 4, p. 250, v. 76. Jayavarman VII "possessed the purified earth, which could be said to be his home"; *IC,* vol. 2, p. 177, v. 70.
84. George Coedès, *IC,* vol. 4, p. 253, v. 25.
85. Minoru Hara, "The King as a Husband of the Earth (mahī-pati)", *Asiatische Studien* 27, no. 2 (1973): 97–114.

references to these extraordinary kingly marriages would be of no particular interest were it not for two reasons.

The first reason is that Chou Ta-kuan, the Mongol envoy to Angkor in 1296, recorded that the Khmers believed that their ruler slept every night with a serpent princess (*nagī*) and that the result of the union was the country's prosperity.[86] Bosch sees the union as replicating a god's ambrosia-producing marriage with his *śakti*.[87] Following J. Ph. Vogel, he also notes that Vāc's aquatic associations helped to shape the imagery of the *nagī*, while *nāgas* and *nagīs* have strong affinity to the imagery of the lotus.[88] Chou Ta-kuan's account of the royal union with a *nagī* was made only about a century later than the two royal marriage inscriptions I have just mentioned. Perhaps the "underworld" in Yaśovarman's inscription, though the poet's chance to illustrate royal glory, is another echo of an indigenous Khmer belief that the king enjoyed a ritually beneficent relationship with a *nagī* below the surface of the soil, from which fertilizing forces were released which guaranteed the earth's productivity. Folk religion may have complemented a royal tantric ritual that made the king the equivalence of Śiva and therefore of the supreme manifestation of creative processes.

The other reason that the twelfth and early thirteenth century references to royal marriages may have more than ordinary interest is that, according to Quaritch Wales, the basement of a royal mountain-temple in Angkor contains a representation of the underworld behind a wall. The "underworld" is adorned with bas-relief of its inhabitants, including *nāgas*.[89]

The language of Yaśovarman's inscriptions may have been influenced by tantric conceptions of divine kingship in the ninth century. Unfortunately the Angkorian inscriptions tell us practically nothing about royal initiation rites.[90] References occur, however, to other forms of ritual and evoke the purification theme in Yaśovarman's inscriptions. Rulers are occasionally described as performing purification ceremonies, sacrifices, and recitation rites. In the ninth century an Indian came to Cambodia for the "purification of the country".[91] Yaśovarman's lake was certainly a zone of purity

86. F.D.K. Bosch, *The Golden Germ*, p. 92.
87. Ibid.
88. Ibid., pp. 136–37.
89. H.G. Quaritch Wales, *The Universe Around Them. Cosmology and Cosmic Renewal in Indianized South-east Asia*, pp. 117–18.
90. On initiation rites at Angkor, see K. Bhattacharya, op. cit., pp. 72, 102.
91. George Coedès, *IC*, vol. 4, p. 42, v. 14. Epigraphic references to sacrifices and recitations are sufficiently frequent to suggest that the rulers performed these

in the neighbourhood of the city; its banks were reserved for religious occasions.[92]

A study of the ritualistic aspects of Angkorian kingship would be worthwhile. Michael Aung Thwin has recently mentioned a growing tendency among younger scholars to see changes of rulers not as events requiring the entire regeneration of all the links in the cosmic chain of power but rather as regeneration accomplished by rites of great antiquity.[93] His view has an important bearing on the study of continuities in earlier Southeast Asian history, though we need not attach too much weight to the disturbing influence of king-making adventures in societies where kinship systems gave more importance to personal prowess than to lineage claims. Performance rather than ancestry provided the criteria for evaluating behaviour in public life and also for entrusting would-be rulers with ritualistic observances on which the well-being of all social classes, especially the farmers, depended. The issue of calendars, with auspicious dates for agricultural ceremonies, was an obviously important annual ritual.[94]

In this chapter I have not been concerned with subregional literary cultures as such, which cannot be discussed when only a single genre of writing in each culture is considered, Javanese eulogistic inscriptions, Vietnamese prose poetry (*phú*) and inscriptions, and Malay Muslim literature would have to be taken into account. Instead, I have tried to look behind the scene at something which is actually happening: writing to produce meaning through literary effects. I have continually examined literary formulations that used conventions such as metaphors, equivalences, contiguous language, intensified language, hyperbole, sets of signifying associations, and structure. These are some of the devices which enabled literary statements to be made and be discovered by textual analysis. Obviously, I have not exhausted the possibilities for studying the Vietnamese poems and Yaśovarman's inscriptions, and I am certain to have made mistakes.

I was interested in how prince Phũ, familiar with the Vietnamese poetic convention that the Tãn Viên mountain was always visible, intensifies the effect by contrasting Tãn Viên's brightness with the

---

responsibilities very seriously. See, for example, *IC*, vol. 1, p. 213, v. 62 and vol. 3, p. 52, v. 17 (sacrifices); vol. 1, p. 213, v. 56 and vol. 4, p. 223, v. 40 (recitations).

92. See note 78 for the view that the lake was an instance of "theocratic hydraulic works" and no more.

93. Michael Aung Thwin's review of Wales' *The Universe Around Them*, in *JAS* 39, no. 3 (1980): 663.

94. George Coedès, *IC*, vol. 2, p. 23, note 4.

wind-swept colours awaiting the envoy on his way back to China. I have also noted how the Vietnamese used a special language to embellish their "mountains and rivers" and distinguished their landscape from what lay across the Chinese borders. I observed that a number of landscape poems conformed to a structure and a set of signifying words, especially in describing the spirits' abode in the clouds. Space, mystery, and timelessness seemed to have helped the poets express their elation. Yaśovarman's Sanskrit inscriptions interested me for the same possibilities. The poets' initial convention of an equivalence between certain signifiers, drawn from Indian imagery, and what the signifiers could mean in a Khmer context enabled them to make a statement about their Śiva-like king. The inscriptions also contained divine metaphors for honouring the king's glory; his glory could be compared with Arjuna's. The king's Śiva-like status, however, is unqualified by metaphor and therefore undiminished.

The two studies in Appendices B and C reflect their authors' concern with language usage. The Javanese poet seeks to embellish the natural scene with language so that he can animate the divine presence immanent in nature but concealed from the eye. The poet writes in a state of poetic rapture comparable with a yogic trance. Day, as Mabbett has done, gives guidance for understanding how the Old-Javanese poems should be read as texts. In Day's words, the landscape is "a setting for poetic composition which does not refer to the natural world but to the processes of poetic writing". The autonomy of the literary process cannot be better demonstrated. The processes in question include maximum use of "verbal ornamentation" (*alaṃkāra*), the device in Indian poetics which Coedès thought was being used as bombast in twelfth-century Cambodian inscriptions.

In Errington's discussion of the Malay *hikayat* the point of interest seems to be the prominence given to sound effects in literature intended to be read aloud. The language of politeness and courtly speech is conveyed by the association of sounds. We can assume that every writer I have mentioned was interested in sound effects. In Java, the vocalization of the written word is certainly an indispensable contribution to good poetry.

I have tried to explain what I mean when I refer to the study of the earlier literatures of Southeast Asia. I have broached, and no more, a line of enquiry which may in time help to delineate particular literary cultures in the region and illustrate the phenomenon of cultural diversity.

Should a historian concern himself with textual studies? I can speak only for myself. The texts noted in this chapter strengthen my expectation that the approach I referred to earlier as "localization" requires one to give thought to the "something else" in local statements which contain foreign materials. The Vietnamese and Khmers were localizing nothing less than two foreign languages, but this need not mean that nothing else can come to light in their literary statements. On the other hand, my interest in textual studies may seem to create a distance between myself and what concerned me in the first half of the essay, where my focus was on assigning a suitable shape to history in earlier Southeast Asia. The distance does not make me uncomfortable. Historical processes are part of the historian's business, and, when one tries to study literary processes, one can be sure that one is dealing with things actually happening when the poet is writing.

I hope, however, that I do not create a distance between myself and fellow historians. I doubt it. Though I have been looking at the texts for their own sake, I have also considered possibilities of changing literary conventions and asked why this should be so. The localization of the Chinese magical islands to heighten the sensation of elation during the second half of the fourteenth century may throw additional light on the extent to which the poets perceived the peril engulfing their country and on the poignant situation of conservatives living in changing times. I am now more interested in what historians have to say about purification rituals and folk religion in Cambodia and elsewhere. I agree with Day's remark that "attending to how poems are written leads one further into rather than away from history".[95] Textual discoveries will always supplement knowledge obtained in other ways. Textual study, though time-consuming, can yield products of history whose processes have been susceptible to investigation and, for that reason, are themselves processed. The products are likely to be culturally more authentic than many types of evidence from the past because they reflect what Jonathan Culler calls "natural" in that they articulate the vision and values assumed to be natural in a culture.

95. Letter to the author, dated 12 February 1981.

CHAPTER SIX

Conclusion

The essay has set forth difficulties which would arise if I were to attempt to write a history of earlier Southeast Asia. It also reveals what some may regard as tendencies diverting me from my obligations as a historian. Circumstances in the part of the world where I happen to study and teach are to some extent responsible for these tendencies.

The field as we know it today exists because teachers and students draw on the work of three groups of scholars. The earliest group worked for many decades before the Second World War when the field, by and large, was occupied by scholars in the archaeological departments of colonial governments in Southeast Asia, and seniority brought them the responsibility of programming research objectives in their respective territories. What Coedès wrote of them deserves to be remembered with respect: "They can scarcely be blamed for having followed the example of the Renaissance philologists and humanists in making the collection and publication of both textual and archaeological source material their first task, and proceeding from there to use the material for establishing a valid chronological framework. Only now can the possibility be envisaged of using the material for other purposes — namely, for providing sociological and economic data with which to fill in the framework and present a more complete picture."[1] These scholars created the field, and we are all in their debt even though what they published may sometimes need to be verified today.

The second group comprises the ever-growing number of historians in the Southeast Asian countries since the end of the Second World War. As D.G.E. Hall observed nearly twenty years ago, "under the stimulus of nationalism the peoples of Southeast Asia

1. G. Coedès, *The Making of South East Asia,* p. vii.

have been history-minded as never before",[2] and nothing that has happened since would have changed his mind. New materials and highly scholarly re-interpretations of old materials are frequently published in books and articles, communicated to seminars, and incorporated in national histories. The western teacher is well aware that his lectures must be revised year by year to take this body of scholarship into account.

The third group, to which I belong, is represented by a very small number of teachers in the non-Southeast Asian universities where, in the United States at least, the so-called "classical" period of Southeast Asian history is usually treated as a brief introductory background in courses which emphasize contemporary or near-contemporary Southeast Asia. The consequence is that hardly any students become interested in earlier Southeast Asia for its own sake.

Outside the discipline of history, however, the state of Southeast Asian studies, from which the past is not excluded, is dramatically different. Those who study and teach anthropology, art history, government, linguistics, and musicology have no difficulty in accommodating their interests under the rubric of Southeast Asian studies, and this development, more than anything else, is keeping interest in the region alive in American universities. The reason for the promising situation is that scholars outside the discipline of history are able to relate their particular expertise in a Southeast Asian subregion to their discipline's wider concerns and show how their discipline benefits from bringing Southeast Asian studies to the fore.

For example, Donn Bayard, drawing on the results of current research in northeastern Thailand and northern Vietnam, believes that prehistory in this part of the world has considerable significance in understanding prehistoric developments in general. Diffusionism, according to him, is now an insufficient explanation for agricultural and technological change.[3] The discipline of anthropology has been enriched by the study of the kinship basis of Southeast Asian cultural systems. The study of settlement patterns and cultures in tropical riverine terrains and the unusual problems such terrains create for

2. D.G.E. Hall, *Historians of South East Asia*, p. 2.

3. Donn Bayard, "The Roots of Indochinese Civilisation", pp. 109–10. One should also bear in mind that Vietnamese archaeologists are throwing new light on folk memories of the past before the Chinese occupation and preserved in fourteenth century tales. Legends about the Hùng kings had their origins in the Vĩnh Phú area of northwestern Vietnam, where numerous sites of the early metal age are being excavated. This development provides new directions for cross-disciplinary research on the borderlands of prehistory and history.

historical archaeology and cultural history will, as the SPAFA (Seameo Project in Archaeology and Fine Arts) seminar on Sriwijaya foresaw in 1979, require innovative interdisciplinary research, including the skills of the natural sciences.[4]

A hospitable approach to Southeast Asian studies has been demonstrated by a political scientist whose own field is outside the region. Quentin Skinner has reviewed a cultural anthropologist's study of the Balinese *nagara* in the nineteenth century and argues that the study is an opportunity for learning something of interest to a "wide range of social scientists and political philosophers". According to Skinner, the *nagara* offers an alternative conception of the meaning of political authority and exercise of power and challenges the parochial assumption in western political theory that ceremonies in public life can never be the real basis of a state. He even enquires whether "our inherited tradition of political analysis may now be serving to inhibit rather than clarify our understanding not merely of alien cultures but also of our own".[5]

Southeast Asian studies are gradually establishing themselves as a necessary part of a liberal arts education in not a few American universities, and nowhere may the results be more immediate and exciting than in the fields of art and music, where very personal ways of seeing and hearing, inherited from Western cultures, can be improved. Art in Southeast Asia was never a socially marginal activity; instead, it throve in communities where religion, work, and political life as well as art belonged to interrelated complexes of experience. For the undergraduate, brought up to assume that art is recreational and tends to be museum-bound, learning to see unfamiliar things through the eyes of the Southeast Asian artist and especially learning something of the processes of artistic production are bound to be educational benefits which may remain with him

---

4. *Seameo Project in Archaeology and Fine Arts. Final Report. Workshop on Research on Sriwijaya* (Jakarta, 1979).
5. Quentin Skinner's review of *Negara: The Theatre State in Nineteenth Century Bali*, by Clifford Geertz (Princeton University Press, 1981), in *The New York Review of Books* 28, no. 6 (16 April 1981): 35–37. Benedict Anderson suggests that his analysis of the Javanese conception of Power and politics may be of some value for political analysis outside Java or Indonesia as it would help to elucidate Weber's concept of "charisma". Weber focused his attention on situations of stress and crisis in social, economic, and political conditions, in which charismatic leaders emerged. Anderson prefers to look for signs of Power in the character of particular cultures, which have to be approached in historical terms. In Southeast Asia, asceticism may signify Power; see Anderson, "The Idea of Power in Javanese Culture", *Culture and Politics in Indonesia*, pp. 64–69.

through life.[6] Again, Javanese gamelan music is often heard in the United States, but its role is not just to provide enjoyment. Musicologists are interested today in the ingredients of music such as pitch, time, timbre, and form and in presenting and analysing the ingredients in the historical and cultural settings of musical traditions. The *laras* (harmony, key, tone modulations) of the gamelan offers a perspective on pitch organization other than what we are accustomed to call "scale", and Western musical experience is enhanced when the Javanese perspective is introduced to the classroom.[7] Learning something of Southeast Asian art and music calls for an unusual degree of participation, and this is precisely why these subjects are beginning to be included as part of a liberal arts education. One day, textual studies in the field of the Southeast Asian literatures may make a similar contribution.

These are some examples of disciplines other than history which have an interest in Southeast Asia and its past. The historian can only be pleased that his field, seen from outside, is not entirely an academic backwater. But this promising situation is not in itself a case for studying earlier Southeast Asian history in a Western university environment. Can the case be strengthened in addition to the argument that, in a shrinking world, civility and the exigencies of the present require attention to be paid to the history of a substantial proportion of the world's population? The historian can bear a few things in mind.

He can remember that the field is still relatively young. Its foundations are not so firmly settled that a great deal of knowledge can now be taken for granted. Even modes of periodization present problems. Connections between causes and effects are still too hypothetical to be made with confidence. Guidelines for studying continuities and changes are speculative. New pieces of evidence can suddenly shake one's favourite reconstructions. The field therefore remains wide open for re-thinking, and here, in my opinion, may be its strength as a teaching subject. The historian is normally the only person who can linger over source materials in order to engage students in classroom discussion. Few teachers of earlier Southeast Asian history have the advantage of discussing their own research with students possessing the necessary language training for studying sources in depth, but my experience is that, even in translation, Pigeaud's *Java in the fourteenth century*, for example, stimulates the intelligent student to read source

---

6. I have drawn on Stanley J. O'Connor's lecture on "Seeing with Southeast Asian art", delivered at Elmira College in 1980.
7. I thank Martin F. Hatch for this information.

materials very carefully and ask sensible questions. This kind of participatory enterprise can, under guidance, endow the field with freshness and a vision of endless possibilities on a scale that no textbook can achieve.

The field lends itself to discussion rather than to teaching from the shoulder in the misplaced belief that a blurred record can somehow be knocked into shape. Moreover, because the field is essentially something to be discussed, students in a liberal arts environment have opportunities for bringing into play the various study tools to which their education in other classrooms is introducing them and especially tools acquired in courses on Southeast Asia within other disciplines. This is why I believe that the notion of local cultural statements containing "something else", to which foreign materials are calling attention, is a helpful one. The interests of historians and non-historians alike can converge on cultural differences which, though never divisive, preserved a rich span of subregional identities. The merit of the approach is illustrated in Japanese history, where students of the Mahāyāna know that their research is also bringing a "something else" that is Shinto into sharper relief and varies according to the part of Japan being studied. [8]. The search for the "something else" in the histories of the Southeast Asian subregions has far to go, and the historian will be in the centre of the undertaking because he, unlike his colleagues in other disciplines, is, or should be, familiar with the progress of studies in a number of subregions and can be alert in spotting scope for informed comparisons. Above all, if I may recall Mary Wright's words once more, only the historian can expect to open up "general ranges" of recorded experience in the Southeast Asian subregions.

And so I end by repeating what I said in the introduction. The interest of the field and also its educational justification is that it provides an opportunity for learning how to learn. In particular, the field is concerned with identifying and understanding historical processes, and here, in my opinion, is its pedagogical value. The historian John Higham neatly describes the style of the historian who is interested in the study of processes when he says: "The process-oriented scholar enjoys the pursuit of truth more than the possession of it". This type of scholar can be distinguished from his product-oriented colleague, who "cares more about the completeness or the coherence of his work than he does about its replication or extension by others. He is unappreciative of negative findings, intolerant of

8. I am grateful to Allan G. Grapard for discussing the evolution of Shinto-Buddhism in the Tendai tradition.

theoretical claims, and unwilling to risk the waste (for him) of time and effort that may be involved in methodological experimentation. He seeks to construct relatively self-sufficient finished products".[9] The present state of earlier Southeast Asian historical studies is such that we are bound to belong to the company of process-oriented scholars, and this means that we and our students have to keep as close as possible to the subregional sources, treated as cultural texts, and forego efforts for the time being to delineate a shape to regional history.

But the reader will recall that my aim in this essay was to provoke discussion. I hope that my terms of reference have been sufficiently broad for this purpose and broad enough to bring what I have neglected into prominence.

9. I quote from Michael Kammen, "On Predicting the Past: Potter and Plumb", *Journal of Interdisciplinary History* 7 (Summer 1974): 115–16.

Appendices

APPENDIX A

Miscellaneous notes on "soul stuff" and "prowess"

I became interested in the phenomenon of "soul stuff" when I was studying the "Hinduism" of seventh-century Cambodia and suspected that Hindu devotionalism (*bhakti*) made sense to the Khmers by a process of self-Hinduization generated by their own notions of what Thomas A. Kirsch, writing about the hill tribes of mainland Southeast Asia, calls "inequality of souls".[1] Among the hill tribes, a person's "soul stuff" can be distinguished from his personal "fate" and the spirit attached to him at birth. "Both the internal quality and the external forces are evidence of his social status".[2] The notion of inequality of souls seems to be reflected in the way the Khmer chiefs equate political status with different levels of devotional capacity.

I then began to observe that scholars sometimes found it necessary to call attention to cultural elements in different parts of the lowlands of Southeast Asia which seemed to be connected with the belief that personal success was attributable to an abnormal endowment of spiritual quality. For example, Shelly Errington in her forthcoming book, *Memory in Luwu*, chapter I, discusses what constitutes a "person" in Luwu, South Sulawesi. In Luwu society, *sumange'* is the primary source for animating health and effective action in the world, and *kerre'* ("effect") is the visible sign of a dense concentration of *sumange'*. Potent humans and also potent rocks, for example, are said to be in "the state of *kerre'* (*makerre'*)". *Sumange'* is associated with

1. Thomas A. Kirsch, *Feasting and Social Oscillation: Religion and Society in Upland Southeast Asia*, p. 15.
2. Ibid., pp. 13–15.

descent from the Creator God and signified by white blood, but this is not always so. Individuals with remarkable prowess can suddenly appear from nowhere, and the explanation is that they are *makerre*. *Kerre* is not invariably contingent on white blood.

In Bali the Sanskrit word *sakti* ("spiritual energy") is associated with Viṣṇu. Viṣṇu represents *sakti* engaged in the world, and a well formed ancestor group is the social form required to actualize *sakti*.[3] But *sakti* in Bali is not related to immobile social situations, for Viṣṇu's preferred vehicle is "an ascendant, expanding ancestor group".[4] Such a group is led by someone of remarkable prowess.

Benedict Anderson, in his essay on "The Idea of Power in Javanese Culture", does not refer to "soulstuff"; his focus is on Power, or the divine energy which animates the universe. The quantum of Power is constant, but its distribution may vary. All rule is based on the belief in energetic Power at the centre, and a ruler, often of relatively humble origins, would emerge when he showed signs of his capacity for concentrating and preserving cosmic Power by, for example, ascetic practices. His feat would then be accompanied by other visible signs such as a "divine radiance".[5] The Javanese notion of the absorption of cosmic Power by one person presupposes that only a person of unusual innate quality could set in motion processes for concentrating cosmic Power by personal effort. On the other hand, the Power this person could deploy in his lifetime inevitably tended to become diffused over the generations unless it was renewed and reintegrated by the personal efforts of a particular descendant.

Anderson's analysis may recall the situation I seemed to detect in seventh-century Cambodia. In both instances ascetic performance distinguished outstanding men from their fellows, and in Luwu as well as in Java visible signs revealed men of prowess and marked them out as leaders in their generation.

Again, according to Vietnamese folklore, the effect of a personal spiritual quality is suggested by the automatic response of local tutelary spirits to a ruler's presence, provided that the ruler had already shown signs of achievement and leadership. A local spirit is expected to recognize and be attracted by a ruler's superior quality and compelled to put himself at such a ruler's disposal.

I have introduced the topics of "soul stuff" and "prowess" in a discussion of the cultural matrix, and we can suppose that these and other indigenous beliefs remained dominant in the protohistoric

---

3. Boon, *The Anthropological Romance of Bali*, pp. 204–5.
4. Ibid., p. 203.
5. Benedict Anderson, "The Idea of Power in Javanese Culture", pp. 1–69.

period in spite of the appearance of "Hindu" features in documentary evidence. I take the view that leadership in the so-called "Hinduized" countries continued to depend on the attribution of personal spiritual prowess. Signs of spiritual quality would have been a more effective source of leadership than institutional support. The "Hinduized" polities were elaborations or amplifications of the pre-"Hindu" ones.

Did the appearance of Theravāda Buddhism on mainland Southeast Asia make a difference? Historians and anthropologists with special knowledge must address this question. I shall content myself with noting a piece of evidence brought to my attention by U Tun Aung Chain which refers to the Buddhist concept of "merit". The Burman ruler Alaungmīntayā of the second half of the eighteenth century is recorded as having said to the Ayudhyā ruler: "My *hpon* (derived from *puñña*, or "merit") is clearly not on the same level as yours. It would be like comparing a garuda with a dragon-fly, a naga with an earthworm, or the sun with a fire-fly". Addressing local chiefs, he said: "When a man of *hpon* comes, the man without *hpon* disappears". Here is Buddhist rendering of superior performance in terms of merit-earning in previous lives and the present one, and we are again dealing with the tradition of inequality of spiritual prowess and political status. Are we far removed from other instances of spiritual inequality noted above? The king's accumulated merit had been earned by ascetic performance; the self had to be mastered by steadfastness, mindfulness, and right effort, and only persons of unusual capacity were believed to be able to follow the Path consistently and successfully during their past and present lives. Such a person in Thailand would be hailed for his *pāramī*, or possession of the ten transcendent virtues of Buddhism. A Thai friend tells me that *pāramī* evokes *bhakti* ("devotion"), and the linguistic association suggests a rapport comparable with what is indicated in seventh-century Cambodia and in Vietnamese folklore about the tutelary spirits.

In all the instances I have sketched, beliefs associated with an individual's spiritual quality rather than with institutional props seem to be responsible for success. Perhaps de la Loubère sensed the same situation in Ayudhyā at the end of the seventeenth century when he remarked: "the sceptre of this country soon falls from hands that need a support to sustain it".[6] His observation is similar to that of Francisco Colin in the Philippines in the seventeenth century:

6. De la Loubère, *A New Historical Relation of the Kingdom of Siam* (reproduced by the Duopage Process in the U.S.A.), p. 107.

"honoured parents or relatives" were of no avail to an undistinguished son.

Others may wish to develop or modify the basis I have proposed for studying leadership in the early societies of Southeast Asia. Explanations of personal performance, achievement, and leadership are required to reify the cultural background reflected in the historical records, and this in turn requires study by historians and anthropologists, working in concert, of the indigenous beliefs behind foreign religious terminology.

APPENDIX B

Six Vietnamese poems of the second half of the fourteenth century

1
Lines written when wandering on the Phật Tich mountain

Chanting and whipping his horse, the poet climbs the lofty ridge.
Treading the monastery grounds, I remove myself from the world's clamour.
Waves of pine sway in the wind and chill the grotto's mouth.[1]
The primeval spirit draws a silken girdle around the mountain's waist.
Among the numberless peaks in the mist are the Three Islands of the spirits.
Among the myriad pipes and drums [of nature] are the nine parts of [Thiều's = Shun's] music.
Let us talk no more of Master Tù-'s marvels.[2]
Roaming everywhere, I have stopped chanting and am now playing my flute.

Phạm Su-Mạnh, *Tho-văn Lý-Trần*, vol. 3, p. 93.

2
Lines written at the grotto on the Bão Phúc cliff in the Hiệp mountain

Bão Phúc, a magic grotto, is above the blue sea.
Today, with official leave, I have been free to roam.
Phu-o-ng Hô and Viên Kiệu appear through the clouds.
Tũ- Phũ and Thanh Dô are floating over the water.[3]

1. Grottos signify supernatural mystery. See Schafer, *The Vermilion Bird*, p. 144, on their Taoist associations in China. Grottos were "the ante-chambers of holy worlds and subterranean paradises." Phạm Su-Mạnh uses the word "grotto" to intensify the mystery of the Phật Tich mountain in his first couplet in parallel verse.
2. Master Tù- is Tù- Dao Hanh, an eclectic twelfth century Buddhist and also a magician. He lived for some time in the Thiên Phúc monastery on this mountain.
3. Tũ- Phu and Thanh Dô are references to the toponyms associated with the abode of the Celestial Emperor, where wondrous music, alluded to in poem 6, is heard. The references are from *The Book of Lieh-tzũ*.

The world's most marvellous sight is the rising of the sun at Du-o-ng Cốc.
The purest air of the rivers and mountains is Bạch-Đằng's autumn.
As I versify I wish to ask old Cát Tiên.[4]
Whether he will give me a half share of these green mountains.

Phạm Su-Mạnh, *Tho-văn Lý-Trần*, vol. 3, p. 106.

3
Lines written on the Hoa cliff in Đông Triều

It thrusts itself into the blue heavens like a jade lotus.
A magnificent scene through the ages. This heroic coastal province!
Bamboo shadows and blossom shade. A green-screened monastery.
Immortals have fashioned and spirits carved a palace among the white clouds.
To the north I am girded by Vạn Kiếp like a range of chilled halberds.
To the south I am held by the Xuân river like a gushing crystalline rainbow.
In the setting sun and leaning on my stick at the high look-out point,
The invigorating air of the mountains and streams fills my breast.

Phạm Su-Mạnh, *Tho-văn Lý-Trần*, vol. 3, p. 108.

4
Visiting Côn mountain

A tall bamboo on the mountain top pierces through the cloud mist.
I glance behind me at the defilement of the world. The road has separated me from it by great distance.
The sound of the spring after the rain is the flow of splashing water.
The mountain air when the sky clears is transparently clear.
Throughout lifetime in the fleeting world, men are all phantasms.
After half a day of stolen leisure, I am indeed an immortal.

---

4. Cát Tiên (Ko Hung) was a Chinese Taoist of the fourth century who sought the ingredients of the elixir of life. See Schafer, *The Vermilion Bird*, pp. 87–88. Ko Hung is supposed to have hoped to find what he wanted in Vietnam but was unable to go there. Phạm Su-Mạnh is claiming equality with the Chinese magician; both have access to the supernatural forces of the universe.

After my elation passes, I want to make my way to the monk's courtyard and spend the night.
The evening bell speeds on the moon and poises it in front of the peak.

Nguyễn Phi Khanh, *Thơ văn Lý-Trần*, vol. 3, p. 423.

5
The Tiên Du monastery

Tiên Dú-c's mountains and rivers. The former [Lý] emperors' capital.
The setting of this famous monastery is sublime. Indeed, it is a little Phu-o-ng Hồ.
In the world of men where are there no traces?
In vain one asks of the immortals what has survived or disappeared.

Nguyễn Phi Khanh, *Thơ văn Lý-Trần*, vol. 3, p. 481.

6
Rising early at the Thiên Thánh Hụ-u Quốc monastery

This palace tower of the company of immortals seems near to Bồng Lai.
The ear hears the music at Heaven's zenith. I easily awaken from my dream.[5]
I rise from sleep on this spring morning without a care.
The wind from the east [the spring wind] is in the courtyard. I watch the blossom open.

Nguyễn Phi Khanh, *Thơ văn Lý-Trần*, vol. 3, p. 474.

5. "The music at Heaven's zenith" alludes to a passage in the *Shih-chi* about an invalid who dreams that he ascends to the heavens. When he reaches the Celestial Emperor's palace in the heavenly heights, he hears wondrously beautiful music.

APPENDIX C

Kakawin and *Hikayat*

Zoetmulder has examined the *manggala* verses which introduce the Old-Javanese *kakawins*, or poetry written in Indian metres.[1] The verses were written as acts of worship in honour of a god and Zoetmulder is able to show that the poet's prayer for divine guidance is uttered in a Javanese cultural setting. The *manggalas* contain the word *dewāśraya*, the literal Sanskrit meaning of which is "having recourse to a god". In Java, however, the loan word signifies "seeking union with the deity", and this is why the poet is writing. Poetry was a yoga exercise.[2] Thus, poets sometimes described their works as "literary temples"[3] in the sense that a god would descend into a poem when the poet's mystical contemplation during the act of writing was intense enough to infuse his poetic language with divinity in the same way that intense worship animated a temple image. Here is a Javanese attitude towards poetry, and Zoetmulder remarks that, "as regards literary yoga, it should be noted that the characteristic form of the *manggala* in Old-Javanese *kakawins*, from which we have deduced its existence, seems to have been unknown in Sanskrit literature".[4]

The *kakawins* belong to a devotional genre of writing. They are written under the influence of a personal religious experience, and the poets use the language they deem "natural" for the experience. The linguistic evidence of what was "natural" is found in language used for poeticizing their wanderings in the countryside. According to Zoetmulder, the linguistic terms for "wandering" are often those normally used for ascetics "in quest of saintliness or supernatural power", and two of the terms have a double meaning: "to seek death by letting oneself be carried away by a stream" and also giving oneself up entirely to "aesthetic pleasure".[5] Landscape can be rendered in religious language because divinity, no matter what name the god of the poet's devotion bears, is immanent in all forms of beauty. To experience beauty means to be in union with the divinity in a trance-like rapture, and the rapture is expressed in the language

1. P.J. Zoetmulder, *Kalangwan. A survey of Old Javanese Literature.*
2. Ibid., pp. 177–78.
3. Ibid., p. 185.
4. Ibid., p. 180.
5. Ibid., p, 171.

of landscape poetry.[6] What is actually seen in nature does not reveal the immanent divinity. Only a poet can sense divinity, and his poem has to capture and celebrate what is concealed from the eye. He does so by means of elaborate linguistic equivalences, and this is why the "literariness" of the *kakawins*, including their sound effects, strives to embellish the natural scene in order to produce the presence of its concealed divinity. The beauty of language rather than of nature itself reveals the vision and the ecstasy of the aesthetic experience. The language is of one who "is able to sense the approach of that mystical union with the divinity in which all consciousness of the self vanishes".[7] And so one poet of the Old-Javanese period writes under the influence of yogic rapture that he is able "to bud forth sprouts of beauty because yoga unites him with the god who is beauty itself".[8] In this state of rapture, a poet hopes that his poem may be a temple to receive the god of beauty. "May Kāma receive his *candi* (temple) from me when I pursue the quest for beauty at the tip of my writing-style [stylus]".[9] Language and not scenery creates beauty.

A.J. Day, another student of Javanese literature, has defined very exactly how these texts should be read. The poet's literary purpose is not with what is natural about the Javanese landscape. Landscape is "a setting for poetic composition which does not refer to the natural world but to the processes of poetic writing".[10]

Day has recently examined the "ornamentation" and "embellishment" which continued to be distinctive features of Javanese literature into the nineteenth century.[11] He, as Zoetmulder does, notes that "verbal ornamentation", known in Sanskrit poetics as *alaṃkāra*, was already a prominent feature in the earliest Old-Javanese poetic text, written on an inscription from Central Java and dated 856. De Casparis, who edited the inscription, observes that the poet's description of a recently planted tree in a temple compound displays ornamentation that "goes far beyond the discrete limits fixed by the classical poets of India".[12] In 1365, almost exactly five hundred years after this inscription was composed, Prapañca acknowledges the same convention when he writes that the Majapahit king enjoyed reading and re-reading a temple's bas-relief which "is illuminating a

6. On "rapture" (langö, etc.), see ibid., pp. 172–73.
7. Ibid., p. 184.
8. Ibid., p. 179.
9. Ibid., p. 185.
10. A.J. Day, *Meanings of Change in the Poetry of Nineteenth-Century Java*, p. 71.
11. Ibid.
12. De Casparis, *Prasasti Indonesia II*, p. 285; and Zoetmulder, *Kalangwan*, p. 230.

language ornament, a *kakawin*".[13] Prapañca himself may be practising the same technique when he refers to the crowds of women awaiting the arrival of touring princes:

> Those whose houses were far away there tried to get at high trees.
> Dangling in bunches from their branches were girls, old and young, [like] luxuriant [fruit].[14]

Zoetmulder's study provides a vivid example of one genre of writing in a local literature. The attention he pays to the significance of words and to the use of language for producing the feeling of rapture rather than describing the external scene belongs to the apparatus of textual study. His chapter entitled "The world of the poem" shows a similar concern with language effects by means of metaphors and similes. For example, he is examining equivalences when he says that "under the guise of Sanskrit personal and place names the poet is presenting a picture of his own country and his own society".[15] By considering figures of speech, Zoetmulder is able to make a general observation of considerable interest. The Old-Javanese poet's depiction of the relationship between man and nature shows "that he saw this world in a way that was connatural to him and his audience: namely essentially as one".[16] Here is one way in which a cultural ambience can be explored.

When we study Javanese poetry we are, as it were, present when something is actually happening: the poets are creating divine beauty in a state of rapture. We know from other sources that tantric meditation was practised in Javanese society, though we cannot assume that tantric yoga meant the same to the Javanese as it did to the Indians.[17] But being in the presence of those who are meditating, as we are when we study how they produced language meaning, is more worthwhile than merely knowing that yogic meditation was practised in Java. Zoetmulder's textual study makes this possible.

To the best of my knowledge, no other earlier Southeast Asian literature has been studied in this way. Shelly Errington's discussion of the Malay *hikyat* genre of literature should, however, be mentioned.[18] Wilkinson defines *hikayat* as "a tale, a history, a narrative,"

---

13. Pigeaud, *Java in the fourteenth century,* vol. 3, canto 32, stanza 4.
14. Ibid., canto 59, stanza 6.
15. Zoetmulder, *Kalangwan,* pp. 187–88.
16. Ibid., p. 214.
17. Ibid., pp. 179–80.
18. Shelly Errington, "Some comments on Style in the Meanings of the Past", *JAS* 38, no. 2 (1979); 231–44.

while Errington defines it more precisely as a written text to be recited in court. Her study is based on the use of language.

These prose texts contain a great deal of material strung together paratactically and often repetitively. The paratactic effect is assisted by the absence of tense in the Malay language, and Errington cites A.L. Becker's observation that certain Austronesian languages do not use a "narrative presupposition" to produce coherence in texts. The *hikayats* were drawn from conventional stories and episodes, and Errington suggests that images from the visible world were brought into being simply by the use of words. The words were listened to for their sounds rather than read. *Hikayats* were written to be recited. Their contents therefore took the form of sounds, and they produced a particular effect. The effect was no less than the experience of listening to the spoken Malay language, a language (*bahasa*) which was essentially the language of politeness. Language defined the shape of human relations; polite behaviour was synonymous with addressing people properly. One result was that nothing induced self-esteem more than hearing one's name mentioned frequently, and so "name" (*nama*) also signified "reputation". *Nama* was nowhere more enhanced than when it was heard or acquired in the context of the ruler's service. Thus, the *hikayats* reflected a preoccupation with being spoken about not only in the present but in the future as well. Indeed, Errington suggests, "the desire to be spoken about, for one's *nama* to be mentioned in other countries and by people in the last age, becomes what we can only translate as a 'motive' for action".[19]

Errington's analysis was presented to a symposium on Southeast Asian attitudes towards the past, and her conclusion was that the *hikayat*'s purpose was not to record the past but to perpetuate it. "One begins to feel, in reading *hikayat*, that the idea that the world is real and words or language artificial is reversed in traditional Malaya where, if anything, *bahasa* was real, solid, present, and almost palpable, while the world was something which would not endure."[20]

One can suppose that, because language registered social behaviour on the Malay Peninsula or in those parts of the archipelago where the language was spoken, the Malay raja in this cultural *maṇḍala* would feel at home when he listened to Malay texts resonant with the sounds of polite language. If Old-Javanese literature is the product of meditative achievement and the poetry of nature is more beautiful than the landscape itself, Malay literature may be read as language schooling for raja society in an anonymous landscape.

---

19. Ibid., p. 242. The significance of *nama* in traditional Malay court society is discussed in A.C. Milner, *The Malay Raja*, pp. 206–18.
20. Ibid., p. 242.

Bibliography

Abdullah, Taufik. *Sejarah Lokal di Indonesia*. Gadjah Mada University Press, 1979.

Aeusrivongse, Nidhi. "*Devarāja* Cult and Khmer Kingship at Angkor". *Explorations in Early Southeast Asia: The Origins of Southeast Asian Statecraft*. Papers on South and Southeast Asia, edited by Kenneth R. Hall and John K. Whitmore, no. 11. Michigan, 1976.

Andaya, Barbara. "The Indian *saudaga raja* in traditional Malay courts". *Journal of the Malaysian Branch of the Royal Asiatic Society* 51, no. 1 (1978).

Anderson, Benedict. "The Idea of Power in Javanese Culture". In *Culture and Politics in Indonesia*, edited by Claire Holt et al. Cornell University Press, 1972.

Atmodjo, M.M. Sukarto K. *The Charter of Kapal*. Aspek-aspek Arkeologi Indonesia, no. 2 (1977).

Barth, A. and A. Bergaigne. *Inscriptions sancrites du Cambodge et Champa* (*ISCC*). Paris, 1885.

Bayard, Donn. "The Roots of Indochinese Civilisation". *Pacific Affairs* 51, no. 1 (1980).

______. "Comment". *Early South East Asia. Essays in Archaeology, History and Historical Geography*, edited by R.B. Smith and W. Watson. Oxford University Press, 1979.

Benda, Harry J. "The Structure of Southeast Asian History". *Journal of Southeast Asia History* 3, no. 1 (1962).

Bhattacharya, K. *Le Religions Brahmaniques dans l'Ancien Cambodge*. EFEO. Paris, 1961.

Boisselier, Jean. *La Statuaire du Champa*. Paris, 1963.

Boon, James A. *The Anthropological Romance of Bali 1597–1972*. Cambridge University Press, 1977.

______. "The Progress of the Ancestors in a Balinese Temple-Group (pre-1906–1972)". *Journal of Asian Studies* 34 (1974).

Bosch, F.D.K. "Notes archéologiques. IV. Le temple d'Angkor Vat". *Bulletin de l'École Française d'Extrême-Orient* 32 (1932).

______. *The Golden Germ. An Introduction to Indian Symbolism.* 's-Gravenhage, 1960.

Brakel, L.F. *The Hikayat Muhammad Hanafiyyah.* The Hague, 1975.

Brandon, James R., ed. *On Thrones of Gold. Three Javanese Shadow Plays.* Harvard University Press, 1970.

Braudel, Fernand. *The Mediterranean and the Mediterranean World in the Age of Philip II.* 2 volumes. Harper Colophon Books, Harper Torchbook edition, 1976.

Bronson, Bennet. "Exchange at the Upstream and Downstream Ends: Notes Toward a Functional Model of the Coastal State in Southeast Asia". In *Economic and Social Interaction in Southeast Asia: Perspectives from Prehistory, History and Ethnology,* edited by Karl L. Hutterer. Michigan Papers on South and Southeast Asia, no. 13, 1977.

______. "The Late Prehistory and Early History of Central Thailand with special reference to Chansen". In *Early South East Asia. Essays in Archaeology, History and Historical Geography,* edited by R.B. Smith and W. Watson. Oxford University Press, 1979.

Bronson, Bennet and Jan Wisseman. "Palembang as Srivijaya: The Lateness of Early Cities in Southern Southeast Asia". *Asian Perspectives* 19, no. 2 (1978).

Brown, C.C., trans. "The Malay Annals". *Journal of the Malaysian Branch of the Royal Asiatic Society* 25, no. 2–3 (1952).

Brugmans, Henri. "Un historien regarde l'intégration européenne". In *Sciences humaines et intégration européenne.* Leiden, 1960.

Buchari. "Epigraphy and Indonesian Historiography". In *An Introduction to Indonesian Historiography,* edited by Soedjatmoko et al. Cornell University Press, 1955.

Bùi Bićh. *Hoàng Việt thi tuyên.* HM2214 in the library of the Societe Asiatique, Paris.

Chatterji, B.R. *History of Indonesia.* 3rd ed. Meerut, 1967.

Chhabra, B.Ch. *Expansion of Indo-Aryan Culture.* Delhi, 1955.

Coedés, George. "La stèle de Prasat Komnap". *Bulletin de l'École Française d'Extrême-Orient* 32, no. 1 (1932).

______. *Les Inscriptions du Cambodge (IC),* 8 volumes. Paris, 1937–1966.

______. *The Indianized States of Southeast Asia.* Honolulu: East-West Center Press, 1968.

______. *The Making of South East Asia.* Translated by H.M. Wright. University of California Press, 1966.

Colless, Brian E. "Were the gold Mines of Ancient Java in Borneo?"

The Brunei Museum Journal 3, no. 3 (1975)

Cortesão, A., ed. *The Suma Oriental of Tomé Pires*, vol. 1. London: The Hakluyt Society, 1944.

Cowan, C.D. and O.W. Wolters, ed. *Southeast Asian History and Historiography. Essays presented to D.G.E. Hall.* Ithaca: Cornell University Press, 1976.

Culler, Jonathan. *Saussure.* Second impression. Fontana Modern Masters, Fontana Paperback, 1979.

______. *Structuralist Poetics. Structuralism, Linguistics, and the Study of Literature.* Reprint. Cornell University Press, 1978.

Davidson, Jeremy H.C.S. "Archaeology in Northern Viet-Nam since 1954". In *Early South East Asia. Essays in Archaeology, History and Historical Geography*, edited by R.B. Smith and W. Watson. Oxford University Press, 1979.

Day, A.J. "Meaning of Change in the Poetry of Nineteenth-Century Java". Ph.D. dissertation, Cornell University, 1981.

de Casparis, J.G. Historical Writing on Indonesia (Early Period)". In *Historians of South East Asia*, edited by D.G.E. Hall (London, 1961).

______. *Indonesian Palaeography. A History of Writing in Indonesia from the Beginning to c. A.D. 1500.* Leiden, 1975.

______. "Pour une histoire sociale de l'ancienne Java principalement au Xème s", *Archipel* 21 (1981).

______. *Prasasti Indonesia*, II (Bandung, 1956).

de Saussure, Ferdinand. *Course in General Linguistics.* McGraw Hill Book Company, 1966.

Diskul, M.C. Subhadradis. "Chedi at Wat Keo Chaya, Suratthani". *Journal of the Malaysian Branch of the Royal Asiatic Society* 53, no. 2 (1980).

Emmerson, Donald K. "Issues in Southeast Asian History: Room for Interpretation — a Review Article". *Journal of Asian Studies* 40, no. 1 (1980).

Errington, Shelly. "Some Comments on Style in the Meanings of the Past". *Journal of Asian Studies* 38, no. 2 (1979).

Filliozat, J. "Le Symbolisme du Monument de Phom Bakheng". *Bulletin de l'École Française d'Extrême-Orient* (*BEFEO*) 44, no. 2 (1954).

______. "Notice sur la vie et les travaux de M. George Coedes". *Bulletin de l'École Française d'Extrême-Orient* 57 (1970).

Finot, L. "Notes d'épigraphie XI: Les inscriptions de Mi-so-n". *Bulletin de l'École Française d'Extrême-Orient* 4 (1904).

Frankel, Hans H. "Classical Chinese". In *Versification: major language types*, edited by W.K. Wimsatt. New York University Press, 1972.

Gaspardone, E. "L'inscription du Ma-Nhai". *Bulletin de la Société des Études Indochinoises* 46, no. 1 (1971).

Gesick, Lorraine. "Kingship and Political Integration in Traditional Siam". Ph.D. thesis, Cornell University, 1976.

Ghoshal, U.N. *A History of Indian Political Ideas*. Reprint. Oxford University Press, 1966.

Gonda, J. *Aspects of Early Visnuism*. Second edition, Motilal Banarsidass, 1969.

______. *Sanskrit in Indonesia*. Nagpur, 1952.

Graves, Elizabeth and Charnvit Kaset-siri. "A Nineteenth Century Siamese Account of Bali: With Introduction and Notes". *Indonesia* 7 (1969).

Hà Văn Tân. "Nouvelles recherches préhistoriques et protohistoriques au Vietnam". *Bulletin de l'École Française d'Extrême-Orient* 68 (1980).

Hall, D.G.E. *Historians of South East Asia*. Edited by D.G.E. Hall. Oxford University Press, 1961.

Hall, Kenneth. "Khmer commercial development and foreign contacts under Sūryavarman I". *Journal of the Economic and Social History of the Orient* 18, no. 3 (1975).

Hara, Minoru. "The King as a Husband of the Earth (mahī-pati)". *Asiatische Studien* 27, no. 2 (1973).

Harrisson, Tom and Stanley J.O 'Connor. *Gold and Megalithic Activity in Prehistoric and Recent West Borneo*. Southeast Asia Program, Data Paper No. 77, Cornell University, 1970.

Hart, Donn V. *Compadrinazgo, Ritual Kinship in the Philippines*. Northern Illinois University Press, 1977.

Harvey, G.E. *History of Burma*. Frank Cass & Co. Ltd., 1967.

Hatch, Martin F. "Lagu, Laras, Layang. Rethinking Melody in Javanese Music". Ph.D. thesis, Cornell University, 1980.

Hawkes, David. *A little Primer of Tu Fu*. Oxford University Press, 1967.

Hawkes, Terence. *Structuralism and Semiotics*. University of California Press, 1977.

Hooker, M.B. *A Concise Legal History of South-East Asia*. Oxford: Clarendon Press, 1978.

Hooykaas, C. *The Old-Javanese Rāmāyaṇa*. Academie van Wetenschappen, Amsterdam. Afdeling voor de Taal-, Letter-, Geschiedkundige en Wijsgeerige Wetenschappen. Verhandelingen. Nieuwe reeks 65, no. 1 (1958).

______. *Religion in Bali*. Iconography of Religions XIII, no. 10. Leiden, 1973.

Hutterer, Karl L. "Prehistoric Trade and the Evolution of Philippine Societies: A Reconsideration". *Economic and Social Inter-*

action in Southeast Asia: Perspectives from Prehistory, History and Ethnology, edited by Karl L. Hutterer. Michigan Papers on South and Southeast Asia, no. 13 (1977).

Huỳnh Sanh Thông, ed. and trans. *The Heritage of Vietnamese Poetry.* Yale University Press, 1979.

Ileto, Reynaldo C. *Magindanao, 1860–1888: The Career of Dato Uto of Buayan.* Data Paper no. 82, Southeast Asia Program, Cornell University, 1971.

______. *Pasyon and Revolution. Popular Movements in the Philippines, 1840–1911.* Ateneo de Manila University Press, 1979.

Jacques, Claude. " 'Funan'. 'Zhenla'. The Reality Concealed by these Chinese Views of Indochina". In *Early South East Asia. Essays in Archaeology, History and Historical Geography,* edited by R.B. Smith and W. Watson. Oxford University Press, 1979.

Jakobson, Roman and Linda R. Waugh. *The Sound Shape of Language.* Indiana University Press, 1979.

Jocano, F. Landa, ed. *The Philippines at the Spanish Contact.* Manila, 1975.

Kahin, George McT. "In Memoriam: Harry J. Benda". *Indonesia* 13 (1972).

Kammen, Michael. "On Predicting the Past: Potter and Plumb". *Journal of Interdisciplinary History* 7 (Summer 1974).

Keesing, Roger M. *Kin Groups and Social Structure.* New York: Holt. Rinehart and Winston, Inc., 1975.

Kirsch, Thomas A. "Complexity in the Thai Religious System: An Interpretation". *Journal of Asian Studies* 36, no. 2 (1977).

______. *Feasting and Social Oscillation: Religion and Society in Upland Southeast Asia.* Data Paper no. 92, Cornell Southeast Asia Program, July 1973.

Krom, N.J. *Hindoe-Javaansche Geschiedenis.* 's Gravenhage, 1931.

Kulke, Hermann. *The Devarāja Cult.* Data Paper no. 108, Cornell Southeast Asia Program, January 1978.

Leach, E.R. *Political Systems of Highland Burma ....* London: G. Bell and Son, 1954, reprinted 1964.

Mabbett, I.W. "Devarāja". *Journal of Southeast Asian History* 10, no. 2 (1969).

______. "Kingship in Angkor". *Journal of the Siam Society* 66, no. 2 (1978).

______. "The 'Indianization' of Southeast Asia: Reflections on Prehistoric Sources". *Journal of Southeast Asian Studies* 8, no. 1 (1977).

______. "The 'Indianization' of Southeast Asia: Reflections on the Historical Sources". *Journal of Southeast Asian Studies* 8, no. 2 (1977).

______. "Varṇas in Angkor and the Indian Caste System". *Journal of Asian Studies* 36 no. 3 (1977).

Manguin, Pierre-Yves. "Études cam II. L'introduction de l'Islam au Campa". *Bulletin de l'École Française d'Extrême-Orient* 66 (1979).

______. "La traversée de la mer de Chine méridionale, des détroits à Canton, jusqu' au 17e siècle (La question des Iles Paracels)". In *Actes du XXIXe Congrès international des Orientalistes*. Paris, 1976.

______. "The Southeast Asian Ship. An Historical Approach". *Journal of Southeast Asian Studies* (*JSEAS*) 11, no. 2 (1980).

Marr, David G. *Vietnamese Anticolonialism*. University of California Press, 1971.

McKinnon, E. Edwards. "Spur-marked Yüeh Type Sherds at Bukit Seguntang". *Journal of the Malaysian Branch of the Royal Asiatic Society* 52, no. 2 (1979).

McVey, Ruth T. *Southeast Asian Traditions. Approaches through Social History*. Yale University Press, 1978.

Matheson, Virginia. "Concepts of State in the *Tuhfat al-Nafis* (The Precious Gift)". In *Pre-Colonial State Systems in Southeast Asia*, edited by Anthony Reid and Lance Castles. Monographs of the Malaysian Branch of the Royal Asiatic Society, no. 6, 1975.

Mendelson, E. Michael. "A Messianic Buddhist Association in Upper Burma". *Bulletin of the School of Oriental and African Studies (BSOAS)* 24, no. 3 (1961).

Milner, A.C. "The Malay Raja: A Study of Malay Political Culture in East Sumatra and the Malay Peninsula in the Early Nineteenth Century". Ph.D. thesis, Cornell University, 1977.

Moron, Eleanor. "Configurations of Time and Space at Angkor Wat". *Studies in Indo-Asian Art and Culture* 5 (New Delhi: International Academy of Indian Culture, 1977).

Mulia, Rumbi. *The Ancient Kingdom of Panai and the ruins of Padang Lawas (North Sumatra)*. Bulletin of the Research Centre of Archaeology of Indonesia, no. 14. Jakarta, 1980.

Nagazumi, Akira. *The Dawn of Indonesian Nationalism. The Early Years of the Budi Utomo, 1908–1918*. Tokyo, 1972.

Nguyễn Phuc Long. "Le nouvelles recherches archéologiques au Vietnam ...". *Arts Asiatiques*, Numéro special, 31 (1975).

Nhá Xuất Bãn Khoa Học Xã Hôi. *Tho-văn Lý-Trần (TVLT)* Vol. 3. Hanoi, 1978.

Noorduyn, J. "The Eastern Kings in Majapahit". *Bijdragen tot de Taal-, Land- en Volkenkunde* 131, no. 4 (1975).

Onghokham. "The Inscrutable and the Paranoid: An Investigation into the Sources of the Brotodiningrat Affair". In *Southeast Asian Traditions. Approaches through Social History*. Yale University Press, 1978.

Osborne, Milton. *River Road to China. The Mekong River Expedition, 1866–73*. New York: Liverright, 1975.

______. *Southeast Asia. An Introductory History*. Sydney: George Allen and Unwin, 1979.

Pigeand, T.G.T. *Java in the Fourteenth Century. A Study of Cultural History. The Nāgara-Kĕrtagāma by Rakawi Prapañca of Majapahit, 1365 A.D.* 5 vols. The Hague, 1960–63.

Rajadhon, Phya Anuman. "The Kwan and its Ceremonies". *Journal of the Siam Society* 50, no. 2 (1962).

Ras, J.J. *Hikajat Bandjar*. The Hague, 1968.

______. "The Panji Romance and W.H. Rasser's Analysis of its Theme". *Bijdragen tot de Taal-, Land- en Volkenkunde* 129, no. 4 (1973).

Renou, Louis. "Sur la structure de kāvya". *Journal Asiatique* 247, no. 1 (1959).

Resink, G.J. *Indonesia's History between the Myths*. The Hague, 1968.

Sarkar, H.B. "A Geographical Introduction to South-East Asia: The Indian Perspective". *Bijdragen tot de Taal-, Land- en Volkenkunde* 137, no. 2–3 (1981).

Schafer, Edward H. *The Vermilion Bird. T'ang Images of the South*. University of California Press, 1967.

Schrieke, B. *Indonesian Sociological Studies, Part 1*. The Hague, 1955.

Schuman, Robert. *Pour l'Europe*, 2e édition, Éditions Nagel Paris, 1964.

Scott. William Henry. "Boat-building and seamanship in classic Philippine Society". Mimeographed, 1979.

Shorto, H.L. "A Mon Genealogy of Kings: Observations on the Nidāna Ārambhakathā". In *Historians of South East Asia*, edited by D.G.E. Hall. Oxford University Press, 1961.

Siegel, James. *Shadow and Sound. The Historical Thought of a Sumatran People*. The University of Chicago Press, 1979.

Skinner, G. William. "Change and persistence in Chinese culture overseas: a comparison of Thailand and Java". *Journal of the South Seas Society* 16, nos. 1–2 (Singapore, 1960).

Smith, R.B. and W. Watson, eds. *Early South East Asia. Essays in Archaeology, History and Historical Geography*. Oxford University Press, 1979.

Soejono, R.P. "The Significance of the Excavation at Gilimanuk (Bali)". In *Early South East Asia. Essays in Archaeology, History and Historical Geography*, edited by R.B. Smith and W. Watson. Oxford University Press, 1979.

Soekmono. "Candi, fungsi dan pengertiannya. Le *candi*, sa fonction et sa conception". *Bulletin de l'École Française d'Extrême-Orient* 62 (1975).

Solheim, Wilhelm G., II. "Reflections on the New Data of Southeast Asian Prehistory: Austronesian Origin and Consequence". *Asian Perspectives* 18, no. 2 (1975).

Stöhr, W. and P. Zoetmulder. *Les religions d'Indonésie*. Paris, 1968.

Sturrock, John, ed. *Structuralism and Since. From Lévi-Strauss to Derrida*. Oxford University Press, 1979.

Suleiman, Satyawati. *A few observations on the use of ceramics in Indonesia*. Aspek-aspek Archeologi Indonesia, no. 7 (1980).

Tambiah, S.J. *World Conqueror and World Renouncer*. Cambridge University Press, 1976.

van Liere, W.J. "Traditional water management in the lower Mekong basin". *World Archaeology* 11, no. 3 (1980).

van Naerssen, F.H. "The Aṣṭādaśavyavahāra in old Javanese". *Journal of the Greater India Society* 15 (1956).

______. *The Economic and Administrative History of Early Indonesia*. Leiden, 1977.

Wales, H.G. Quaritch. *The Making of Greater India*. Second ed. London, 1961.

______. *The Universe Around Them. Cosmology and Cosmic Renewal in Indianized South-east Asia*. London, 1977.

Wang Gungwu. "Introduction". In *Perceptions of the Past in Southeast Asia*, edited by Anthony Reid and David Marr. Published for the Asian Studies Association of Australia by Heinemann Educational Books (Asia) Ltd., Kuala Lumpur, 1979.

Warder, A.K. "Classical Literature". In *A Cultural History of India*, edited by A.L. Basham. Oxford University Press, 1975.

Wheatley, Pual. "Satyānṛta in Suvarṇadvīpa. From Reciprocity to Redistribution in Ancient Southeast Asia". In *Ancient Trade and Civilization*, edited by J.A. Sabloff et al. University of New Mexico Press, 1975.

Wisseman, Jan. "Markets and Trade in Pre-Majapahit Java". In *Economic and Social Interaction in Southeast Asia. Perspectives from Prehistory, History, and Ethnology*, edited by Karl L. Hutterer. Michigan Papers on South and Southeast Asia, no. 13, 1977.

Wolters, O.W. "Assertions of Cultural Well-being in Fourteenth Century Vietnam: Part I". *Journal of Southeast Asian Studies* 10, no. 2 (1979).

______. "Assertions of Cultural Well-being in Fourteenth Century Vietnam: Part II". *Journal of Southeast Asian Studies* 11, no. 1 (1980).

______. Ayudhyā and the Rearward Part of the World". *Journal of the Royal Asiatic Society*, Parts 3 and 4 (1968).

______. *Early Indonesian Commerce*. Cornell University Press, 1967.

______. "Historians and Emperors in Vietnam and China:

Comments Arising out of Lê Văn Hu-u's History, Presented to the Trần Court in 1272". In *Perceptions of the Past in Southeast Asia*, edited by Anthony Reid and David Marr. Published for the Asian Studies Association of Australia by Heinemann Educational Books (Asia) Ltd., Kuala Lumpur, 1979.

———. "Khmer 'Hinduism' in the Seventh Century". In *Early South East Asia. Essays in Archaeology, History and Historical Geography*, edited by R.B. Smith and W. Watson. Oxford University Press, 1979.

———. "Lê Văn Hu-u's Treatment of Lý Thần Tôn's reign (1127–1137)". *Southeast Asian History and Historiography. Essays presented to D.G.E. Hall*, edited by C.D. Cowan and O.W. Wolters. Ithaca: Cornell University Press, 1976.

———. "Northwestern Cambodia in the Seventh Century". *Bulletin of the School of Oriental and African Studies* 37, no. 2 (1974).

———. "Phạm Su-Mạnh's Poems Written when Patrolling the Vietnamese Northern Border in the Middle of the Fourteenth Century". *Journal of Southeast Asian Studies*, in press.

———. "Studying Sriwijaya". *Journal of the Malaysian Branch of the Royal Asiatic Society* 52, no. 2 (1979).

———. *The fall of Śrīvijaya in Malay History*. Cornell University Press, 1970.

Wright, Mary C. "Chinese History and the Historical Vocation". *Journal of Asian Studies* 23, no. 4 (1964).

Yu, Insun. "Law and Family in Seventeenth and Eighteenth Century Vietnam". Ph.D. thesis, University of Michigan, Ann Arbor, 1978.

Zoetmulder, P.J. *Kalangwan. A Survey of Old Javanese Literature*. The Hague, 1974.

THE AUTHOR

Professor O. W. Wolters is Goldwin Smith Professor of Southeast Asian history at Cornell University.

Other titles
by the
INSTITUTE OF SOUTHEAST ASIAN STUDIES

A Colloquium on Southeast Asian Studies
edited by Tunku Shamsul Bahrin, Chandran Jeshurun, and A. Terry Rambo

Southeast Asian Seas: Frontiers for Development
edited by Chia Lin Sien and Colin MacAndrews

Southeast Asian Affairs
An annual review

Conflict and Regional Order in Southeast Asia
by Michael Leifer

Cambodia: A Bibliography
compiled by Zaleha Tamby

State and Society in Thailand, 1767–1873: Transformation of the Economic System
by Hong Lysa

Contemporary Southeast Asia
A quarterly journal